Exploring Azure Container Apps

Scaling Modern and Cloud-Native Apps and Microservices

Naga Santhosh Reddy Vootukuri
Taiseer Joudeh
Wael Kdouh

Apress®

Exploring Azure Container Apps: Scaling Modern and Cloud-Native Apps and Microservices

Naga Santhosh Reddy Vootukuri
Seattle, WA, USA

Taiseer Joudeh
Amman, Jordan

Wael Kdouh
Miami, FL, USA

ISBN-13 (pbk): 979-8-8688-1485-3
https://doi.org/10.1007/979-8-8688-1486-0

ISBN-13 (electronic): 979-8-8688-1486-0

Copyright © 2025 by Naga Santhosh Reddy Vootukuri, Taiseer Joudeh and Wael Kdouh

This work is subject to copyright. All rights are reserved by the Publisher, whether the whole or part of the material is concerned, specifically the rights of translation, reprinting, reuse of illustrations, recitation, broadcasting, reproduction on microfilms or in any other physical way, and transmission or information storage and retrieval, electronic adaptation, computer software, or by similar or dissimilar methodology now known or hereafter developed.

Trademarked names, logos, and images may appear in this book. Rather than use a trademark symbol with every occurrence of a trademarked name, logo, or image we use the names, logos, and images only in an editorial fashion and to the benefit of the trademark owner, with no intention of infringement of the trademark.

The use in this publication of trade names, trademarks, service marks, and similar terms, even if they are not identified as such, is not to be taken as an expression of opinion as to whether or not they are subject to proprietary rights.

While the advice and information in this book are believed to be true and accurate at the date of publication, neither the authors nor the editors nor the publisher can accept any legal responsibility for any errors or omissions that may be made. The publisher makes no warranty, express or implied, with respect to the material contained herein.

    Managing Director, Apress Media LLC: Welmoed Spahr
    Acquisitions Editor: Smriti Srivastava
    Development Editor: Laura Berendson
    Coordinating Editor: Jessica Vakili

Cover image by Pixabay.com

Distributed to the book trade worldwide by Springer Science+Business Media New York, 1 New York Plaza, New York, NY 10004. Phone 1-800-SPRINGER, fax (201) 348-4505, e-mail orders-ny@springer-sbm.com, or visit www.springeronline.com. Apress Media, LLC is a Delaware LLC and the sole member (owner) is Springer Science + Business Media Finance Inc (SSBM Finance Inc). SSBM Finance Inc is a **Delaware** corporation.

For information on translations, please e-mail booktranslations@springernature.com; for reprint, paperback, or audio rights, please e-mail bookpermissions@springernature.com.

Apress titles may be purchased in bulk for academic, corporate, or promotional use. eBook versions and licenses are also available for most titles. For more information, reference our Print and eBook Bulk Sales web page at http://www.apress.com/bulk-sales.

Any source code or other supplementary material referenced by the author in this book is available to readers on GitHub (https://github.com/Apress). For more detailed information, please visit https://www.apress.com/gp/services/source-code.

If disposing of this product, please recycle the paper

Table of Contents

About the Authors xi

About the Technical Reviewer xiii

Acknowledgments xv

Introduction xvii

Chapter 1: Introduction to Azure Container Apps 1

    1.1 Understanding Azure Container Apps 2

        1.1.1 Architecture of Azure Container Apps 4

        1.1.2 Azure Container Apps Use Cases 6

        1.1.3 Key Features and Benefits 10

        1.1.4 Comparison with Azure App Services 12

        1.1.5 Comparison with Azure Kubernetes Service (AKS) 14

        1.1.6 Use Cases and Scenarios 16

        1.1.7 Pricing and Plans 17

        1.1.8 What's Coming Next? 18

        1.1.9 Reference Architecture 20

    1.2 Summary 21

Chapter 2: Deploying First Containerized App to Azure Container Apps 23

    2.1 Setting Up a Development Environment 24

    2.2 Azure Container Registry 25

    2.3 Create the Benefits Manager Backend API 26

    2.4 Understanding the Code Structure 28

TABLE OF CONTENTS

    2.4.1 Enums 28

    2.4.2 Models 28

    2.4.3 Services 31

    2.4.4 Program Configuration 41

    2.4.5 Docker Configuration 44

2.5 Use .http Files in Visual Studio to Validate API 47

2.6 Deploying to Azure Container Apps 48

    2.6.1 Create Azure Infrastructure 48

    2.6.2 Create Log Analytics Workspace and Application Insights 50

    2.6.3 Azure Container Infrastructure 52

    2.6.4 Build and Publish the Docker Image 52

    2.6.5 Deploy to Azure Container Apps 53

2.7 Accessing Published API 55

2.8 Summary 55

Chapter 3: Creating and Deploying Frontend – Blazor Web Application 57

3.1 Setting Up a Development Environment 58

3.2 Introduction to Blazor Framework 59

3.3 Why Blazor for Frontend? 59

3.4 Create Frontend Web App Project 62

3.5 Understanding the Code Structure 63

    3.5.1 ClaimModel.cs Class 63

    3.5.2 Components Layout 64

    3.5.3 ClaimsService.cs 65

    3.5.4 Blazor Components 68

    3.5.5 Program Configuration 78

3.6 Docker Configuration 80

3.7 Creating Azure Infrastructure 82

    3.7.1 Build and Publish the Docker Image.......................................83

    3.7.2 Deploying to Azure Container Apps 84

    3.7.3 Update the Backend Web API Container App Ingress Property.............85

3.8 Summary..88

Chapter 4: Integrating Dapr with Azure Container Apps 89

4.1 Introduction to Dapr 90

4.2 Benefits of Integrating Dapr in Azure Container Apps...................................93

4.3 Configure Dapr on a Local Development Machine 94

4.4 Configure Backend API Locally via Dapr 97

4.5 Configure ACA Web - Frontend Locally via Dapr 100

4.6 Run ACA Web - Frontend and ACA API Backend Locally Using Dapr...........104

4.7 Test ACA Web - Frontend and ACA API Backend Locally Using Dapr...........106

4.8 Debug and Launch Dapr Applications in VS Code 107

4.9 Overview of Dapr State Management API 110

4.10 Use Dapr Client SDK for State Store Management....................................118

    4.10.1 Add Dapr Client SDK to the Backend API Project.............................118

    4.10.2 Create a New Concrete Implementation to Manage Claims Persistence 119

    4.10.3 Register the ClaimsStoreManager New Service and DaprClient......124

4.11 Use Azure Cosmos DB with Dapr State Store Management API................125

    4.11.1 Provision Cosmos DB Resources.......................................125

    4.11.2 Create a Component File for State Store Management 130

    4.11.3 Running Backend and Frontend Application....................................133

    4.11.4 Configure Managed Identities in Container App 136

    4.11.5 Assign the Container App System-Identity to the Built-in Cosmos DB Role...137

TABLE OF CONTENTS

4.12 Deploy Backend API and Frontend Web App Projects to ACA 138
- 4.12.1 Create an ACA-Dapr Component File for State Store Management 138
- 4.12.2 Build Frontend Web App and Backend API App Images in Azure Container Registry 139
- 4.12.3 Add Cosmos DB Dapr State Store to the Azure Container Apps Environment 140
- 4.12.4 Enable Dapr for Both Frontend and Backend Container Apps 140
- 4.12.5 Deploy New Revisions of Both Frontend and Backend Apps to ACA 141

4.13 Summary 141

Chapter 5: Async Communication with Dapr Pub/Sub API 143

5.1 Pub/Sub Pattern with Dapr 143
5.2 Testing Pub/Sub Locally 145
5.3 Setting Up the Backend Background Processor Project 150
- 5.3.1 Create the Backend Service Project 150
- 5.3.2 Docker Configuration 150
- 5.3.3 Add Models 153
- 5.3.4 Install the Dapr SDK Client NuGet Package 153
- 5.3.5 Create an API Endpoint for the Consumer to Subscribe to the Topic 154
- 5.3.6 Register Dapr and Subscribe Handler at the Consumer Startup 157
- 5.3.7 Update Backend API to Publish a Message When a Claim Is Saved ... 162

5.4 Use Azure Service Bus As a Service Broker for Dapr Pub/Sub API 163
- 5.4.1 Create an Azure Service Bus Namespace and a Topic 163
- 5.4.2 Create a Local Dapr Component File for Pub/Sub API Using Azure Service Bus 165
- 5.4.3 Create an ACA Dapr Component File for Pub/Sub API Using Azure Service Bus 166

TABLE OF CONTENTS

5.5 Deploy the Backend Background Processor 170

    5.5.1 Build the Backend Background Processor and the Backend API App Images and Push Them to ACR..170

    5.5.2 Create a New Azure Container App to Host the New Backend Background Processor 171

    5.5.3 Deploy New Revisions of the Backend API to Azure Container Apps 172

    5.5.4 Add the Azure Service Bus Dapr Pub/Sub Component to the Azure Container Apps Environment 172

5.6 Summary...173

Chapter 6: ACA with Dapr Bindings and Scheduled Jobs with Dapr Cron Binding 175

6.1 Interfacing with an External System..176

    6.1.1 Overview of the Dapr Bindings Building Block 178

6.2 Updating the Backend Background Processor Project 183

    6.2.1 Create an Event Handler (API Endpoint) to Respond to Messages Published to Azure Storage Queue 183

    6.2.2 Create the Dapr Input Binding Component File 185

    6.2.3 Create the Dapr Output Binding Component File............................187

    6.2.4 Use Dapr Client SDK to Invoke the Output Binding.........................189

    6.2.5 Test Dapr Bindings Locally 192

6.3 Configure a Dapr Secret Store Component with Azure Key Vault...............195

    6.3.1 Create an Azure Key Vault Resource..195

    6.3.2 Grant Backend Processor App a Role to Read Secrets from Azure Key Vault...196

    6.3.3 Create Secrets in the Azure Key Vault 197

    6.3.4 Create an ACA Dapr Secrets Store Component File.........................198

    6.3.5 Create Input and Output Binding Component Files Matching Azure Container Apps Specs 199

TABLE OF CONTENTS

    6.4 Cron Bindings 201

        6.4.1 Add a Cron Binding Configuration 201

        6.4.2 Add the Endpoint to Be Invoked by Cron Binding 203

        6.4.3 Update the Backend Web API Project 205

        6.4.4 Add Action Methods to the Backend Web API Project 210

        6.4.5 Add Cron Binding Configuration 211

    6.5 Deploy Backend API and Backend Background Processor Projects to ACA 212

        6.5.1 Build Both Projects' App Images and Push Them to ACR 212

        6.5.2 Add the Cron Dapr Component to the ACA Environment 213

        6.5.3 Deploy New Revisions of the Backend API and Backend Background Processor to Azure Container Apps 213

    6.6 Azure Container Apps Jobs 214

    6.7 Summary 215

Chapter 7: Monitoring and Observability 217

    7.1 Azure Container Apps and Application Insights 217

        7.1.1 Application Insights Overview 218

    7.2 Installing Application Insights SDK into the Three Microservice Applications 219

        7.2.1 Install the Application Insights SDK Using NuGet 219

        7.2.2 Set RoleName Property in All the Services 221

        7.2.3 Set the Application Insights Instrumentation Key 230

    7.3 Deploy Services to ACA and Create New Revisions 231

        7.3.1 Add Application Insights Instrumentation Key As a Secret 231

        7.3.2 Build New Images and Push Them to ACR 232

        7.3.3 Deploy New Revisions of the Services to ACA and Set a New Environment Variable 233

    7.4 Visualizing Telemetry Data 234

TABLE OF CONTENTS

7.4.1 Distributed Tracing via Application Map 234

7.4.2 Monitor Production Application Using Live Metrics 235

7.4.3 Logs Search Using Transaction Search 236

7.4.4 Failures and Performance Panels 238

7.5 Summary 239

Chapter 8: Kubernetes Event-Driven Autoscaler (KEDA) 241

8.1 Azure Container Apps Scaling Behaviors 241

8.1.1 Scaling Triggers 242

8.2 Overview of Kubernetes Event-Driven Autoscaler (KEDA) 243

8.3 Configure Scaling Rule in the Backend Background Processor Project 245

8.3.1 KEDA Azure Service Bus Scaler 245

8.3.2 Create a New Secret in the Container App 248

8.3.3 Create a Custom Scaling Rule from Azure CLI 249

8.4 Testing Scaling Rules 251

8.4.1 End-to-End Test to Generate Several Messages 251

8.5 Summary 254

Index 255

About the Authors

Naga Santhosh Reddy Vootukuri works for Microsoft as a Principal Software Engineering Manager in Azure SQL product. He has more than 17 years of experience in designing and developing several products within Microsoft, ranging from SSIS to MDS and currently in Azure SQL DB. He has deep knowledge in cloud computing, distributed systems, artificial intelligence (AI), microservice-based architecture, and cloud-native apps and has experience working in three different Microsoft centers (India, China, and the United States). Santhosh has authored and published numerous research articles in peer-reviewed and indexed journals. He is a core MVB blogger at DZone and an active senior IEEE member handling various conferences as technical chair in the Seattle IEEE region. He also manages several open source projects on GitHub, which have several stars. He frequently speaks and presents at various conferences about AI and cloud computing, and you can contact him on LinkedIn at `https://www.linkedin.com/in/naga-santhosh-reddy-vootukuri-5a67a133/`.

Taiseer Joudeh works for Microsoft Consultation Services as a Principal App Dev Consultant. He has more than 15 years of experience in developing and managing different software solutions for the finance, transportation, logistics, and e-commerce sectors. Taiseer has been deeply involved in .NET development since early framework versions with a deep knowledge of distributed systems, microservices architecture, cloud-native apps, and Microsoft Azure.

ABOUT THE AUTHORS

Wael Kdouh is a seasoned architect with over 20 years of experience developing innovative solutions for leading software companies. He has successfully led the completion of several mission-critical projects in multiple sectors such as airline solutions and retail. Wael holds a PhD in Computer Science from Southern Methodist University (SMU). As a Principal Cloud Architect at Microsoft, Wael spends the majority of his time assisting Microsoft customers with architecting cloud-native applications. In addition, he manages open source projects like APIOps and others. You will find him actively blogging on Medium and occasionally tweeting on X. You can stay in touch with Wael on LinkedIn.

About the Technical Reviewer

As a Cloud Solution Architect for Microsoft's Application Innovation team, **Tommaso Stocchi** helps developers leverage Microsoft's technologies to build cloud-native intelligent applications and implement DevOps practices. He has extensive experience and knowledge in cloud computing and software development.

Acknowledgments

I would like to thank my wife, Sandhya, for supporting me throughout this journey as it involved countless hours of work over the weekends, and she always encouraged me to pursue my dreams. Grateful to my parents and sister. Thanks to my team (SQL deployment – RDM) and my manager (Mohamed El Hassouni) at Microsoft who encouraged and supported me when I told him about my book-writing journey. Finally, lots of love to my kids, Sky and Rio. I also extend my deepest gratitude and thanks to the following people:

- **Wael Kdouh and Taiseer Joudeh:** I sincerely thank my partners and fellow authors of this book; without their support, I couldn't have completed this book on time. Wael lives in Florida and Taiseer is from Jordan, and I am from Seattle. Even though we are in different time zones, we never had any issues in meeting and discussing about the book.

- **Tommaso Stocchi:** Another good friend who is also the technical reviewer of this book, and he works from Italy. He played a key role in providing great feedback about this book, which helped in improving its overall quality. Thank you, Tommaso, and soon we will collaborate on the .NET Aspire book.

- **Smriti and the Apress Team:** I sincerely thank each of you for giving me wonderful opportunities to work with you and with Apress. I have been an active member of the Apress technical reviewing team, and after talking to Smriti, she encouraged and pushed me to pitch in

ACKNOWLEDGMENTS

the idea to pursue my book writing journey. Always grateful to you for trusting me in my capabilities, and today I have completed ten book reviews for Apress.

- **Nirmal Selvaraj:** Thanks for your support in making my work look extraordinary. I appreciate all the emails to discuss and sort out issues promptly.

Lastly, I would like to thank all the people from the C# and Azure developer community, who purchased this book and are reading this page. I hope this book will play a key role in your learning journey of exploring Azure Container Apps with a practical example.

—Santhosh

My deepest gratitude to my wife, Salma Abdeljawad, for her boundless support and understanding. Your steady support and belief in my work were a gift I will always treasure. To my children, Hamza, Zein, and Zeid – thank you for being the light in my life, and for reminding me, in your own special ways, to pause, smile, and keep moving forward.

—Taiseer Joudeh

I would like to extend my deepest gratitude to my wife, Lama Kdouh, whose unwavering support, patience, and encouragement have been the foundation of my journey. A heartfelt thank-you to the incredible leadership at Microsoft, especially Niki Buchanan for her guidance and vision. I'm also immensely grateful to all of my teammates at Microsoft – past and present – whose collaboration and shared knowledge have profoundly shaped my understanding and expertise over the years. This book is as much a reflection of your contributions as it is my own.

Above all, I want to acknowledge my daughter, Mila Kdouh, whose curiosity, joy, and boundless imagination continue to inspire me every day. Her presence reminds me of the importance of dreaming big and staying grounded in love.

—Wael Kdouh

Introduction

Welcome to *Exploring Azure Container Apps*, your definitive guide to mastering the deployment, management, and scaling of containerized applications on Microsoft Azure. In today's fast-paced digital landscape, businesses need to launch applications rapidly and efficiently. Containerization has revolutionized how we package, deploy, and manage applications, offering portability and consistency across various environments. However, as applications grow in complexity, managing and orchestrating numerous containers can become challenging. This book aims to simplify this journey, providing you with a practical, hands-on approach to leveraging Azure Container Apps (ACA) to their fullest potential.

Azure Container Apps is a managed, serverless, Kubernetes-based container runtime designed for building and running cloud-native applications. It allows developers to focus on business logic rather than managing complex infrastructure. Built on top of Kubernetes, ACA simplifies container orchestration, giving you the benefits of Kubernetes without needing to become an expert. This book will guide you through the core concepts, practical implementations, and advanced features of ACA, empowering you to build resilient, scalable, and cost-effective applications on Azure.

Throughout this book, we'll dive deep into various aspects of Azure Container Apps, starting from the fundamentals and progressing to more advanced topics. Each chapter provides a blend of theoretical knowledge and practical exercises, ensuring you not only understand the concepts but also know how to apply them in real-world scenarios. Let's look at what each chapter has in store for you.

INTRODUCTION

Chapter Overviews

- **Chapter 1: Introduction to Azure Container Apps:** This chapter lays the foundation by introducing the core concepts of Azure Container Apps. We'll explore what ACA is, its architecture, and why it's an ideal choice for modern application development. You'll learn about the serverless paradigm, workload profiles (Consumption and Dedicated), and how ACA simplifies container orchestration. We'll also discuss various use cases, such as microservices, event-driven processing, public API endpoints, background processing, and jobs. Finally, we'll compare ACA with Azure App Services to help you understand which service best suits your needs.

- **Chapter 2: Deploying First Containerized App to Azure Container App:** This chapter guides you through deploying your first application to Azure Container Apps. We'll start with an introduction to Azure Container Registry (ACR) and how to push container images. You'll learn how to create a microservice, specifically the Claims Manager API using ASP.NET Minimal APIs, and understand its functionality.

  We'll cover setting up your development environment, creating the underlying Azure infrastructure, and deploying the Claims Manager container app to Azure. This chapter focuses on hands-on experience, ensuring you can deploy your own applications with confidence.

- **Chapter 3: Creating and Deploying Frontend – Blazor Web Application:** Building upon the backend API from Chapter 2, this chapter introduces the frontend web application using the Blazor framework. You'll learn about Blazor, its benefits, and why it's a powerful tool for frontend development. We'll walk you through creating a Blazor project, "BenefitsManager. Frontend.WebPortal.Ui", and deploying it to ACA. You'll also learn how to invoke the backend APIs from the frontend and update the backend APIs' Ingress property to restrict traffic, enhancing security. This chapter provides a complete end-to-end application deployment experience.

- **Chapter 4: Integrating Dapr with Azure Container Apps:** This chapter delves into the Distributed Application Runtime (Dapr) and its integration with Azure Container Apps. You'll learn what Dapr is, its benefits, and how to configure it on your local development machine. We'll cover best practices for Dapr integration and how to decouple the frontend and backend applications locally using Dapr. Additionally, we'll explore Dapr's state management capabilities and provision Azure Cosmos DB as a state store. This chapter introduces advanced microservices patterns and enhances your application's resilience and scalability.

- **Chapter 5: Async Communication with Dapr Pub/Sub API:** In this chapter, we'll explore the Dapr Pub/Sub pattern, enabling asynchronous messaging between microservices. You'll learn how to test the Pub/Sub pattern locally and introduce a new background service, "ACA Processor - Backend," configured for Dapr. We'll use Azure Service Bus as a service broker for the Dapr Pub/Sub API and deploy the background service to Azure Container Apps.

INTRODUCTION

> This chapter focuses on building loosely coupled, event-driven systems that improve application responsiveness and reliability.

- **Chapter 6: ACA with Dapr Bindings and Scheduled Jobs with Dapr Cron Binding:** This chapter covers Dapr bindings and how to schedule jobs using Cron bindings. You'll learn how to interface with external systems, extend the background processor service to interact with an external system, and use Azure Key Vault via a Dapr secret store component to externalize secrets. We'll also explore how the Cron binding can trigger actions and add a Cron binding to the background processor. Finally, we'll deploy the updated background processor and API projects to Azure. This chapter enhances your application's integration capabilities and automation.

- **Chapter 7: Monitoring and Observability:** This chapter focuses on monitoring and observability in Azure Container Apps. You'll learn how ACA integrates with Application Insights to examine application telemetry, configure Application Insights for your microservices, and deploy updated projects to Azure. We'll also understand how telemetry data is visualized, providing insights into your application's health, performance, and usage. This chapter is essential for maintaining and optimizing your deployed applications.

- **Chapter 8: Kubernetes Event-Driven Autoscaler (KEDA):** This chapter discusses ACA's autoscaling behaviors with a focus on the Kubernetes Event-Driven Autoscaler (KEDA).

INTRODUCTION

You'll understand Azure Container Apps scaling behaviors, learn about KEDA, and create a scaling rule for the backend background processor project. We'll also test the scaling of the background processor. This chapter ensures your applications can dynamically adjust to varying workloads, optimizing resource utilization and cost.

By the end of this book, you'll have a solid understanding of Azure Container Apps, its architecture, deployment strategies, advanced features like Dapr and KEDA, and essential practices for monitoring and scaling. This knowledge will empower you to build and manage robust, scalable, and efficient cloud-native applications on the Azure platform. Whether you're a developer, architect, or IT professional, this book will serve as a valuable resource in your journey to mastering Azure Container Apps. I am sure that after reading this book, you will be a better developer and can take advantage of Azure Container Apps in your applications.

CHAPTER 1

Introduction to Azure Container Apps

In today's world, businesses need to launch apps fast and without hassle. The rise in containerization has caused a revolution in how we package, deploy, and manage applications. Containers are movable light packages of app code along with the dependencies it needs to run. They make sure everything stays the same across different setups, from the developers' machines to the production servers.

However, as applications grow in complexity, managing and orchestrating numerous containers across distributed environments can increasingly become challenging. This is where container orchestration comes to the rescue. Container orchestration helps in automating the deployment, scaling, and management of containerized applications. Kubernetes is a widely used container orchestration platform that provides essential capabilities like

1. **Automated Deployment and Scaling**: Easy to deploy and scale applications across multiple containers

2. **Load Balancing**: Distribute incoming traffic efficiently across containers to ensure high availability and performance

3. **Self-Healing**: Automatically restart or replace failed containers to maintain application availability

4. **Service Discovery**: Enables seamless communication between different microservices within a distributed application

1.1 Understanding Azure Container Apps

Azure Container Apps (ACA) is a fully managed, serverless, Kubernetes-based container runtime designed for building and running cloud-native applications. ACA allows developers to focus on business logic rather than managing cloud infrastructure.

At the core, ACA is built on top of Kubernetes, a powerful tool for managing containers. Kubernetes is great for handling complex setups, but it can be difficult to learn. ACA simplifies things, giving you the benefits of Kubernetes without needing to become a Kubernetes expert. This means you can easily deploy and manage your containerized apps, even if you're new to Kubernetes.

The Serverless Paradigm
Azure Container Apps (ACA) leverages serverless architecture, eliminating the need for developers to manage infrastructure. The platform dynamically provides resources based on application load, ensuring efficient resource allocation and cost optimization. By automatically scaling applications in response to real-time traffic, ACA allows developers to prioritize application development and delivery, rather than infrastructure concerns.

ACA's serverless capabilities are further enhanced by **workload profiles**, which provide more control over resource allocation and performance.

Workload Profiles

A workload profile decides how much computing power and memory container apps can be used in an environment.

The **Consumption profile**, which is the default setting, showcases the benefits of serverless computing by automatically scaling your application from zero to handle any incoming traffic, ensuring a pay-as-you-go model.

For more specialized workloads, ACA has **Dedicated profile,** which provides dedicated hardware resources ensuring steady performance and separation from other apps. You can choose from different setups, including general-purpose, memory-focused, and even GPU-powered instances. You can set the lowest and highest number of instances and adjust how scaling works. This allows you to better manage costs and boost performance.

By setting up different profiles, you can adjust the underlying infrastructure to meet your application-specific needs. Managing workload profiles can be done over CLI as well as through the Azure portal, which we will cover in future chapters.

Beyond Infrastructure as a Service (IaaS)

Traditional cloud infrastructure solutions often require developers to manage virtual machines and their associated operating systems and software. While this offers customization, it also adds complexity and maintenance overhead. ACA moves beyond this model, providing a fully managed platform where infrastructure setup and scaling are handled automatically. This empowers developers to focus on their application logic rather than managing virtual machines.

Ideal for Microservices Architectures

The increasing popularity of microservices, where applications are built as a collection of small independent services, has highlighted the advantages of containers. Containers offer a perfect way to package and deploy these services, ensuring they remain isolated and portable and function

CHAPTER 1   INTRODUCTION TO AZURE CONTAINER APPS

consistently across different environments. ACA, with its built-in support for containers, makes it easy for developers to deploy and manage large numbers of microservices, leading to more flexible, scalable, and reliable applications.

1.1.1 Architecture of Azure Container Apps

To fully understand how ACA works, it's important to understand its architecture and the building blocks (see Figure 1-1).

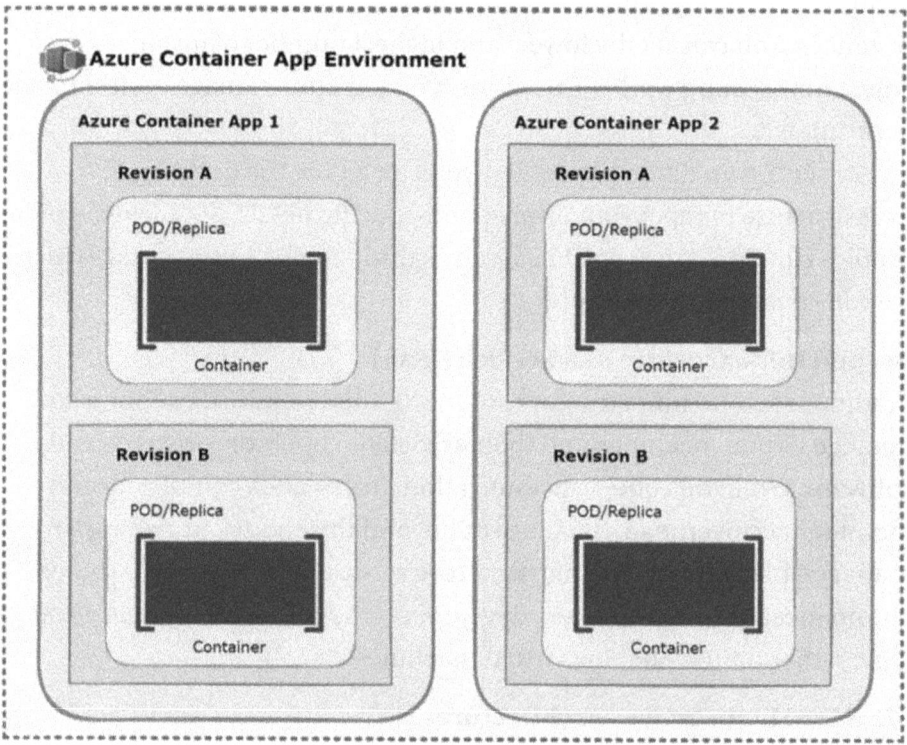

Figure 1-1. *Azure Container Apps architecture (Courtesy: Microsoft)*

CHAPTER 1   INTRODUCTION TO AZURE CONTAINER APPS

1. **Environments**: The Container App Environment is a secure boundary around several container apps. It contains one or more container apps. All container apps within an environment are deployed into a dedicated Azure Virtual Network, which makes it possible for these different container apps to communicate securely. It handles scaling, failover, load balancing for the container apps. In addition, all the logs produced from all container apps in the environment are sent to a dedicated Log Analytics workspace. Log Analytics workspace used to provide monitoring and observability functionality. Each environment will have its own Log Analytics workspace and will be shared among all container apps within the environment.

2. **Container Apps**: This is where the container actually runs. It leverages the resources provided by the environment such as networking, logging, and security. Each container app represents a single deployable unit that can contain one or more related containers. In the Azure portal, container app serves as the entry point for managing the application, revisions, and replicas.

3. **Revisions**: For each container app, you can create up to 100 revisions. Revisions are a way to deploy multiple versions of an app where you have the option to send the traffic to a certain revision. You can select if revision mode will support one or multiple active revisions at the same time to support A/B testing scenarios or canary deployments.

A container app running in single revision mode will have a single revision that is backed by zero-many pods/replicas.

4. **Replica**: These are instances of a revision providing compute and memory to actually run your application. Azure Container Apps can automatically scale out by creating more replicas to handle increased load. The platform supports up to 300 replicas per revision.

5. **Containers**: Containers in the Azure Container Apps are grouped together in pods/replicas inside revision snapshots. A pod/replica is composed of the application container and any required sidecar containers. Containers can be deployed from any public or private container registry, and they support only Linux-based x86-64 (Linux/amd64) images. For Windows container support, refer to this feature request on GitHub: https://github.com/microsoft/azure-container-apps/issues/181.

1.1.2 Azure Container Apps Use Cases

Azure Container Apps offers a flexible platform to support a wide array of application patterns (see Figure 1-2).

CHAPTER 1 INTRODUCTION TO AZURE CONTAINER APPS

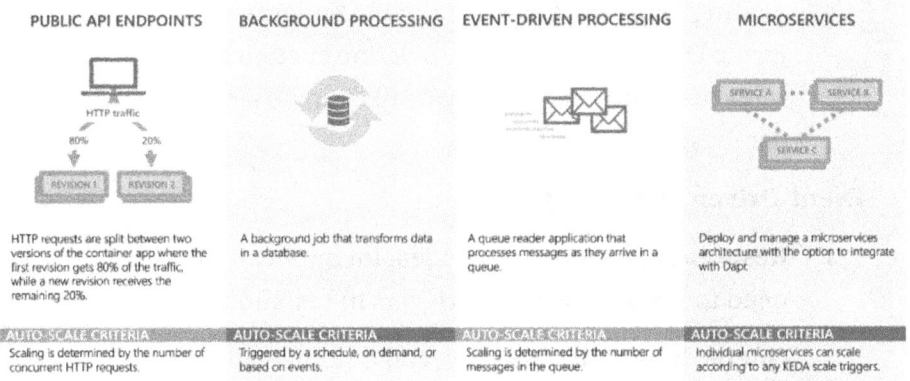

Figure 1-2. Azure Container Apps use cases and scenarios (Courtesy: Microsoft)

Microservices

1. **Decoupled Architecture**: ACA seamlessly supports deploying and managing complex microservices architectures, where applications are broken down into smaller, independent services.

2. **Dapr Integration (Optional)**: For enhanced communication and state management between microservices, ACA offers integration with Dapr (Distributed Application Runtime), an open source, platform-agonistic application runtime designed to simplify the development and management of cloud-native distributed applications.

3. **Independent Scaling**: Each microservice within the ACA environment can scale independently based on its specific needs, optimizing resource utilization.

CHAPTER 1   INTRODUCTION TO AZURE CONTAINER APPS

4. **Scaling Triggers**: Leverage KEDA (Kubernetes Event-Driven Autoscaling) to define custom scaling rules based on various triggers like queue length or database activity.

Event-Driven Processing

1. **Responsive Applications**: Ideal for applications that need to react to events or triggers in real time.

2. **Queue-Based Scaling**: ACA can automatically scale based on the number of messages in a queue, ensuring resources match up to the incoming workload. **Example:** An event processing application that scales up when there's a surge of messages in a queue and scales down during idle periods.

Public API Endpoints

1. **Versioning**: ACA supports deploying multiple revisions (versions) of your container app simultaneously.

2. **Controlled Rollouts**: Traffic splitting allows for gradual rollouts of new versions, directing a percentage of traffic to the new revision while the majority remains on the stable version.

3. **A/B Testing**: Test new features or changes with a subset of users before full deployment.

4. **Scaling Based on Demand**: ACA automatically scales based on the number of concurrent HTTP requests your API receives.

Background Processing

1. **Long-Running Tasks**: Suitable for applications that perform tasks in the background, like data processing or scheduled jobs.

2. **Resource-Based Scaling**: ACA scales based on CPU or memory usage, ensuring adequate resources for your background processes. **Example:** A data transformation application that runs continuously to process data in a database and scales up or down as needed.

Jobs

In addition to running apps, ACA also allows to execute containerized tasks that run for a transient duration and then exit. These tasks are known as **Jobs**. Jobs are ideal for scenarios like automating batch operations, handling event-driven processing, performing scheduled maintenance, and much more. Job executions can be three types:

1. **Manual**: These jobs are initiated on demand, either through the Azure portal, Azure CLI, or by sending a request to ARM API. These are suited for one-time tasks.

2. **Scheduled**: These jobs run on a predefined schedule similar to Cron jobs. Using expressions, we can specify the exact time and frequency. These are ideal for periodic tasks like data cleanup or report generation.

3. **Event-Driven**: These jobs are triggered by events from external sources like changes to Azure blob storage or messages arriving in a queue. ACA leverages KEDA scalers to monitor event sources and automatically start job executions based on predefined rules.

CHAPTER 1 INTRODUCTION TO AZURE CONTAINER APPS

1.1.3 Key Features and Benefits

Azure Container Apps offers a variety of features that make it a compelling choice for businesses looking to modernize their application deployment and management (see Figure 1-3).

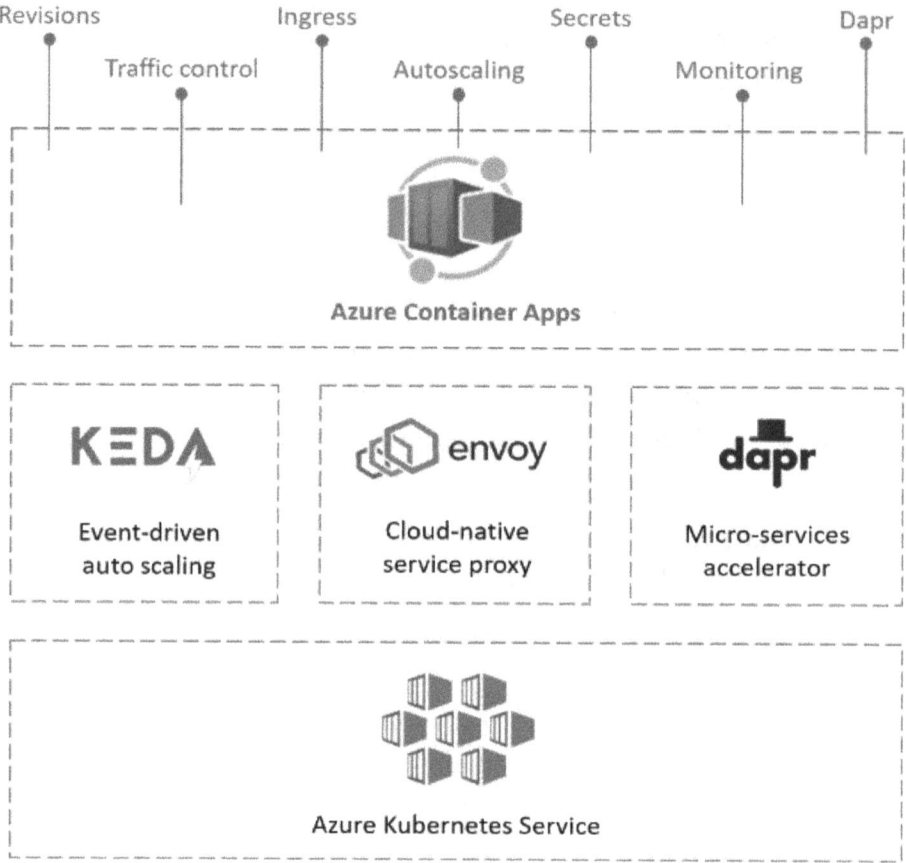

Figure 1-3. *Azure Container Apps powered by Kubernetes and open source technologies*

1. **Serverless Simplicity**: ACA eliminates the need for infrastructure management, allowing developers to focus solely on their applications. The platform automatically scales resources based on demand, ensuring optimal performance and cost-efficiency.

2. **Kubernetes Integration**: ACA harnesses the capabilities of Kubernetes, the leading container orchestration platform, without requiring in-depth Kubernetes knowledge. This enables streamlined deployment, scaling, and management of containerized applications.

3. **Microservices Support**: ACA is inherently suited for microservices architectures, allowing independent deployment and scaling of individual services. The platform supports features essential for microservices communication and management.

4. **Autoscaling**: ACA adapts to changing traffic patterns by automatically scaling the number of running containers. This ensures applications can handle varying loads while maintaining optimal performance and resource utilization.

5. **Built-in Monitoring and Logging**: ACA provides built-in monitoring and logging capabilities through seamless integration with Azure Monitor. This offers real-time insights into application performance, resource usage, and logs, simplifying troubleshooting and optimization.

6. **CI/CD Integration**: ACA seamlessly integrates with popular Continuous Integration and Continuous Deployment tools, automating the build, test, and deployment process for faster and more reliable application updates.

7. **Dapr Integration**: ACA's native support for Dapr (Distributed Application Runtime – an open source, platform-agonistic application runtime designed to simplify the development and management of cloud-native distributed applications). Dapr simplifies the development of microservices applications. Dapr provides building blocks for features like service communication and state management, making it easier to build complex distributed applications.

8. **Open Source**: ACA is built on open source technologies like Dapr, KEDA, and Envoy, fostering transparency and collaboration within the developer community. This allows for greater flexibility and customization options.

1.1.4 Comparison with Azure App Services

Azure Container Apps and Azure App Services both offer strong platforms to host apps in Azure, but they serve different purposes and different development styles. Understanding the differences between these two services will help developers to make informed decisions based on their specific requirements and architectural needs.

- **Deployment Model**: Azure App Services follows a Platform as a Service (PaaS) model. It hides the underlying infrastructure and provides a managed runtime environment for applications. Developers deploy their applications directly to Azure App Services, leveraging its built-in capabilities for scaling, load balancing, and security. On the other hand, ACA emphasizes a container-centric approach, providing greater control and flexibility over the application environment. Developers package their applications into containers and deploy them to ACA, leveraging its container orchestration capabilities.

- **Containers**: Azure App Services supports containerized workloads, allowing developers to deploy Docker-based applications. ACA is built for containers from ground up, offering native support for containerized applications.

- **Scaling**: Azure App Services and ACA both offer autoscaling capabilities like dynamically adjusting resources based on application demand. However, ACA's autoscaling is more granular and tightly integrated with container orchestration. ACA can scale individual containers within an application, providing fine-grained control over resource allocation and optimization.

- **Microservices**: Azure App Services can support microservices architectures; however, ACA is aligned with microservices principles providing natural fit for containerized microservices deployments. ACA's support for service discovery, load balancing, and inter-service communication facilitates the development and deployment of complex microservices applications.

- **Kubernetes**: Azure App Services abstracts away Kubernetes, which shields developers from its complexities. While ACA also abstracts away the complexities of Kubernetes, ACA builds upon its powerful orchestration capabilities while providing a streamlined developer experience. This allows developers to benefit from Kubernetes features without needing to master its complex configurations.

1.1.5 Comparison with Azure Kubernetes Service (AKS)

Azure Kubernetes Service (AKS) offers a managed Kubernetes environment within Azure, providing unparalleled control and flexibility over Kubernetes cluster configuration and management. ACA, while built upon Kubernetes, prioritizes simplicity and ease of use, abstracting away Kubernetes complexities.

- **Kubernetes Expertise**: AKS demands a deeper understanding of Kubernetes concepts and management practices. Developers working with AKS need to be familiar with Kubernetes architecture, configuration, and troubleshooting. ACA, on the other hand, caters to developers who may not have extensive Kubernetes expertise. ACA's simplified interface and abstractions allow developers to deploy and manage containerized applications without delving into the intricacies of Kubernetes.

- **Control**: AKS grants developers fine-grained control over Kubernetes cluster configuration and management. Developers can customize their

Kubernetes clusters, install add-ons, and configure networking and security policies. ACA, on the other hand, offers flexibility in application configuration and deployment while abstracting away many of the low-level Kubernetes configurations.

- **Virtual Network (VNet) Integration**: AKS provides full VNet integration and custom networking options, which enables developers to configure network policies as needed. ACA also allows integration with virtual networks; however, this must be configured only at the time of creating the ACA environment.

- **Serverless**: ACA aligns with serverless principles, automatically scaling applications and managing infrastructure based on demand. AKS, while offering autoscaling capabilities, requires more explicit configuration and management. Developers working with AKS need to define autoscaling rules and monitor cluster resources to ensure optimal utilization.

POINT TO NOTE

AKS is ideal for scenarios where you need granular control over Kubernetes and its configurations.

ACA allows developers to focus on their application logic rather than Kubernetes management, thereby accelerating development cycles and reducing operational overhead.

1.1.6 Use Cases and Scenarios

Azure Container Apps is an ideal platform for a wide range of use cases and scenarios, spanning from simple web applications to complex microservices architectures.

- **Web Applications**: ACA offers a scalable and high-performing environment for web applications. Automatic scaling ensures your application gracefully handles sudden spikes in demand, and Azure Monitor integration provides real-time performance insights. You can even use custom domains and SSL certificates to maintain your brand and ensure security.

- **Web APIs**: ACA excels at deploying and managing containerized APIs, seamlessly integrating with other Azure services and allowing for secure access control. Integration with Microsoft Entra ID adds another layer of security through robust authentication and authorization.

- **Microservices**: Built with microservices principles in mind, ACA is the perfect platform for deploying and managing containerized microservices. Service discovery, load balancing, and seamless inter-service communication simplify the creation of complex microservices applications. ACA's autoscaling ensures each microservice can scale independently based on demand, optimizing resource usage and costs.

- **Event-Driven Applications**: With support for triggers and bindings, ACA empowers you to build applications that react to events from various Azure services or external systems. You can configure triggers to activate your ACA containers in response to HTTP requests, queue messages, or even timer events.

- **Background Tasks**: ACA reliably handles background tasks and batch processing, optimizing resource utilization. Using Jobs, you can schedule your containers to run at specific intervals or trigger them based on events.

1.1.7 Pricing and Plans

Azure Container Apps offers two pricing plans:

- **Consumption Plan**: This serverless option bills only for the resources your application actively uses, calculated based on vCPU-seconds, gigabyte seconds (for memory), and the number of requests processed. It also provides a generous free tier that includes 180,000 vCPU-seconds, 360,000 GiB-seconds, and 2 million requests per month. After exceeding the free tier, you pay $0.000024 per vCPU-second during active usage and even less during idle usage. Requests are billed at $0.40 per million after the initial 2 million free requests.

- **Dedicated Plan**: This plan utilizes dedicated hardware tailored to your needs, offering predictable costs. You pay per instance, and the price varies depending on the chosen configuration (e.g., CPU, memory, GPU). For example, a high-performance instance with 32 vCPUs and 128 GB RAM can cost over $2,500 per month.

> **POINT TO NOTE**
>
> The Consumption plan is generally a cost-effective choice for applications with variable workloads or those that can scale to zero during idle periods. The Dedicated plan is suitable for applications demanding consistent performance, resource isolation, or specialized hardware configurations, despite its higher cost.

1.1.8 What's Coming Next?

This book offers a hands-on, practical application built using a microservices architecture pattern. The application centers around an expense management solution, enabling external users (employees) to submit expenses, which are then reviewed by internal users (administrators). The solution will consist of multiple microservices, each with specific capabilities, demonstrating how ACA, Dapr, and KEDA can simplify microservice-based architectures.

The diagram below shows the architecture of the solution that we will build throughout the book's chapters (see Figure 1-4).

The main components of the solution are as follows:

- **ACA Web App Frontend** is a simple ASP.NET Blazor Server app that accepts requests from external users to manage their expenses, and it allows internal users to review submitted expenses. It invokes the component "ACA Web API-BFF" endpoints via HTTP or gRPC.

- **ACA Web API BFF** is a minimal backend Web API that contains the business logic of expenses management service, data storage, data retrieval, and publishing messages to the Azure Service Bus Topic.

CHAPTER 1   INTRODUCTION TO AZURE CONTAINER APPS

- **ACA Processor Backend** is a minimal Web API that functions as an event-driven backend processor. It is responsible for sending emails to expense owners based on messages received from an Azure Service Bus Topic when there are changes in the expense status. Additionally, it handles events from external systems using Dapr Input bindings and triggers external events through Dapr Output bindings.

- **ACA Meilisearch Service** is a minimal backend Web API that hosts the open source lightweight search engine (Meilisearch). It is responsible for storing submitted expenses of external users and allowing full text search for internal users.

- **ACA Job Indexer Service** is a console application deployed as an ACA Job. It is responsible for indexing all submitted expenses and any changes to them into the search engine.

- **ACA Job Scheduled Service** is a console application deployed as an ACA Job, triggered by a CRON schedule (a nightly job). This service is responsible for creating aggregates of the submitted expenses and storing the aggregated data in Azure Redis Cache for future use by a reporting dashboard.

- Autoscaling rules using KEDA are configured in the "ACA Processor - Backend" service to scale out/in replicas based on the number of messages in the Azure Service Bus Topic.

- Azure Container Registry is used to build and host container images and deploy images from ACR to ACA.

CHAPTER 1   INTRODUCTION TO AZURE CONTAINER APPS

- Application Insights and Azure Log Analytics are used for monitoring, observability, and distributed tracings of ACA.

- Authentication and authorization are applied on the ACA Web App Frontend to control who can access the solution and control the available features of the signed-in user.

1.1.9 Reference Architecture

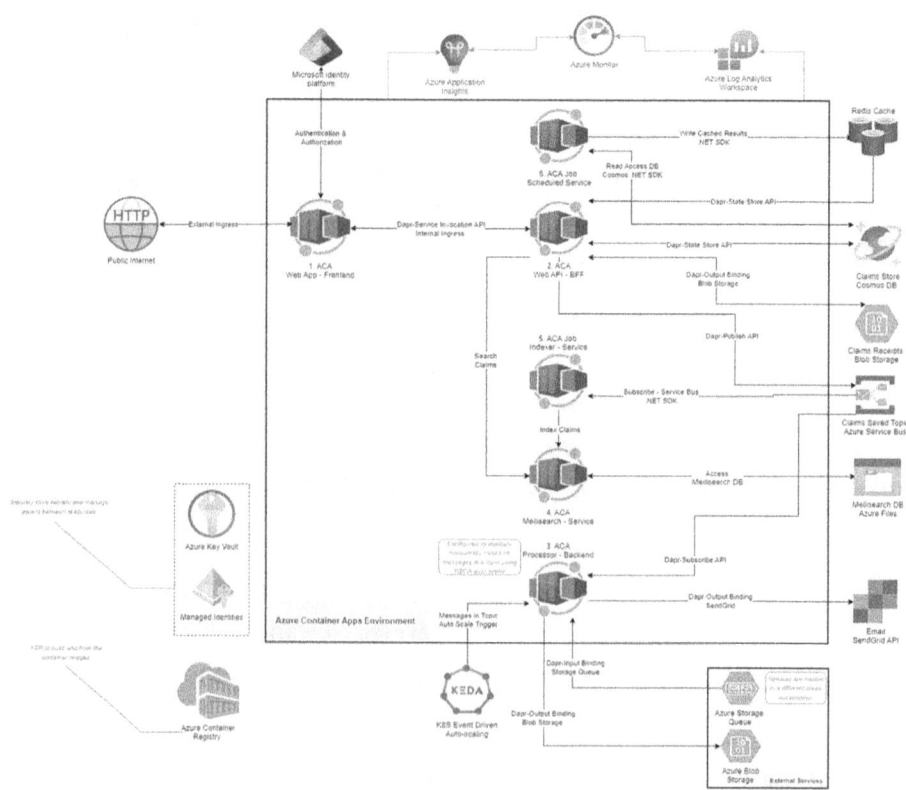

Figure 1-4. Architecture diagram of the Claims application

1.2 Summary

In this chapter, we explored Azure Container Apps, covering their key features, benefits, pricing plans, and how they compare to other Azure services like Azure App Services and Azure Kubernetes Service. We also discussed real-world applications and use cases, highlighting how containers – through their portability and efficiency – are transforming modern software development and deployment. Additionally, we set the stage for a practical exploration of ACA's capabilities with real-world applications. In the upcoming chapters, we will build an application from the ground up, providing a hands-on experience. Buckle up!

… CHAPTER 2

Deploying First Containerized App to Azure Container Apps

In Chapter 1, we looked at the *Benefits Manager* application along with the reference architecture. In this chapter, you will be introduced to the first service, *Claims Manager*, specifically its functionality. We will leverage the ASP.NET minimal API framework to create the first backend API service. The learning objectives for this chapter include the following:

- Introduction to Azure Container Registry and how to push images.

- Create the first microservice ACA API Backend called Claims Manager, which serves as the API for our Claims Application.

- Understand how the Claims Manager service works.

- Explore various tools and technology options used to build the service.

CHAPTER 2   DEPLOYING FIRST CONTAINERIZED APP TO AZURE CONTAINER APPS

- Create the underlying Azure infrastructure.
- Deploy the ACA API Backend container app to Azure.

Let us dive into some prerequisites before we begin!

2.1 Setting Up a Development Environment

Make sure you have your development environment set up and configured by installing or setting up the resources below.

- An Azure account with an active subscription – https://azure.microsoft.com/free/?ref=microsoft.com&utm_source=microsoft.com&utm_medium=docs&utm_campaign=visualstudio
- Dotnet 9.0 or a higher version – https://dotnet.microsoft.com/en-us/download
- PowerShell 7.0 or a higher version (for Windows users only) – https://learn.microsoft.com/en-us/powershell/scripting/install/installing-powershell-on-windows?view=powershell-7.4#installing-the-msi-package
- Docker Desktop – https://docs.docker.com/desktop/install/windows-install/
- Visual Studio Code – https://code.visualstudio.com/
- VS Code Docker extension – https://marketplace.visualstudio.com/items?itemName=ms-azuretools.vscode-docker

- Install the Rest Client Extension for sending HTTP requests and view responses directly inside VS Code – https://marketplace.visualstudio.com/items?itemName=humao.rest-client

- Install the latest version of Visual Studio with the **ASP. NET and web development workload** to get Blazor templates. Visual Studio community edition – https://visualstudio.microsoft.com/vs/community/

- Azure CLI – https://docs.microsoft.com/cli/azure/install-azure-cli

- Git CLI – https://git-scm.com/

2.2 Azure Container Registry

The Azure Container Registry (ACR) is a fully managed Azure service that allows developers to store and manage container images for deployment in any cloud including Azure. ACR offers features that enhance security, scalability, and integration with other Azure services, such as

1. **Integrated Authentication and Authorization:** Supports both Microsoft Entra ID and Managed Identity, allowing secure access to images without requiring credentials.

2. **Geo-Replication:** Ensures high availability by replicating images across multiple regions, making it efficient for global applications needing fast deployment times in various regions.

3. **Build Capabilities:** ACR Tasks allow automated image building and updates, providing a powerful Continuous Integration/Continuous Deployment (CI/CD) capability.

4. **Content Trust:** ACR can enforce image signing, ensuring that only trusted images are pulled and deployed.

5. **Network Configurations:** Supports private endpoints, virtual networks, and firewall rules, helping ensure restricted access for enhanced security.

2.3 Create the Benefits Manager Backend API

In this chapter, we will walk through the process of deploying a containerized application that manages claims for a fictional benefits manager. This application is built using ASP.NET and follows a microservices architecture. We will cover the code structure, the essential classes, and interfaces and how to configure the Azure environment for deployment.

Once you have a development environment up and running, it's time for us to create the first Web API backend service.

You can use Visual Studio UI or CLI to create and initialize a Minimal API project.

Using CLI

Open VS developer command prompt and go to the root folder where you want to create the project/solution and run the command below:

```
dotnet new webapi -minimal -n BenefitsManager.Backend.Bff.Api
```

CHAPTER 2   DEPLOYING FIRST CONTAINERIZED APP TO AZURE CONTAINER APPS

This command will initialize and create an ASP.NET Minimal API project. To add this newly created project to the existing solution, run the below command:

dotnet sln add BenefitsManager.Backend.Bff.Api/BenefitsManager.Backend.Bff.Api.csproj

Using Visual Studio

Open Visual Studio, click on create a new project, and select "ASP.NET Web API" from the list of templates as shown in Figure 2-1. In the next window, unselect the **"use controllers"** option to create Minimal APIs.

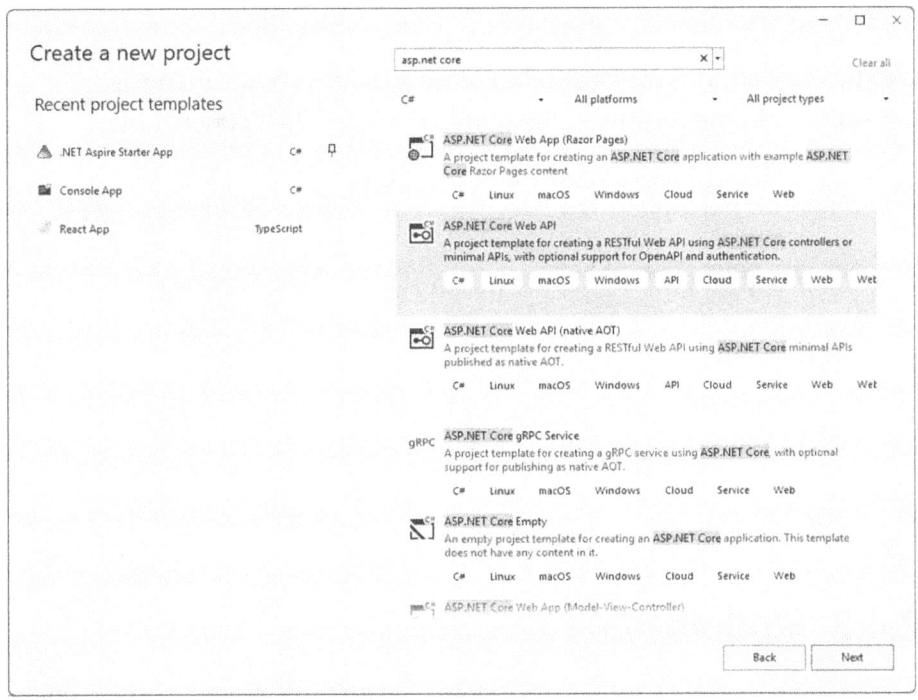

Figure 2-1. *Select the ASP.NET core Web API template from the list*

27

> **POINT TO NOTE**
>
> In the upcoming chapters, we will use VS Code more often since there are few extensions available in VS Code. However, the solution can be opened and run within Visual Studio as well.

2.4 Understanding the Code Structure

2.4.1 Enums

We start by defining the various statuses a claim can have. This is represented in the Enums.cs file that lives under the Common folder.

```
namespace BenefitsManager.Common.Models
{
    public enum ClaimStatus
    {
        Pending,
        Approved,
        Rejected
    }
}
```

2.4.2 Models

In the project root, add a new folder named Models. The folder includes several models representing the data structures we will use. These models located in the "Models" folder include

```
using System.ComponentModel;
using BenefitsManager.Backend.Bff.Api.Common;
```

```csharp
namespace BenefitsManager.Backend.Bff.Api.Models
{
    public class ClaimModel
    {
        public required Guid ClaimId { get; set; }
        public required string Merchant { get; set; }
        public decimal ClaimedAmount { get; set; }
        public decimal? ApprovedAmount { get; set; }
        public long PurchaseDate { get; set; }
        public required ClaimCategoryModel Category { get; set; }
        public string Description { get; set; } = string.Empty;
        public required List<ClaimStatusModel> StatusLog { get; set; }
        public required ClaimStatus CurrentStatus { get; set; }
            = ClaimStatus.Pending;
        public required string ReceiptPath { get; set; }
        public required UserModel CreatedBy { get; set; }
        public long CreatedOn { get; set; }
        public long? ModifiedOn { get; set; }
    }

    public class ClaimCategoryModel
    {
        public required string CategoryCode { get; set; }
        public required string ParentCategoryName { get; set; }
        public required string CategoryName { get; set; }
    }
```

```csharp
public class ClaimStatusModel
{
    public required ClaimStatus Status { get; set; } =
    ClaimStatus.Pending;
    public string? Comment { get; set; }
    public required UserModel SetBy { get; set; }
    public long Ts { get; set; }
}

public class UserModel
{
    public required string Id { get; set; }
    public required string Email { get; set; }
    public required string Name { get; set; }
}

public class ClaimAddModel
{
    public required string Merchant { get; set; }
    public decimal ClaimedAmount { get; set; }
    public long PurchaseDate { get; set; }
    public required string CategoryCode { get; set; }
    public string Description { get; set; } = string.Empty;
    public required string ReceiptPath { get; set; }
    public required UserModel CreatedBy { get; set; }
}

public class ClaimUpdateModel
{
    public required string Merchant { get; set; }
    public decimal ClaimedAmount { get; set; }
    public long PurchaseDate { get; set; }
    public required string CategoryCode { get; set; }
```

```
        public string Description { get; set; } = string.Empty;
        public required string ReceiptPath { get; set; }
    }

    public class ClaimStatusUpdateModel
    {
        public required decimal ApprovedAmount { get; set; }
        public required ClaimStatus NewStatus { get; set; }
        public string Comment { get; set; } = string.Empty;
        public required UserModel SetBy { get; set; }
    }
}
```

2.4.3 Services

The Services folder contains the interface and its implementation for managing claims. **IClaimsManager.cs** interface defines the operations for claims management, and the **FakeClaimsManager.cs** is a mock implementation of the claims manager that uses in-memory lists to simulate database operations. This is an interim solution to quickly spin up a working API. In the upcoming chapters, we will replace in-memory with an actual Cosmos DB. A detailed list of methods and their use cases are shown in Table 2-1.

Table 2-1. *List of operations/methods inside IClaimsManager.cs interface*

Operation	Use Case	Purpose
GetClaimsByCreatorAsync	Fetch all claims created by a specific user	Retrieve a list of claims associated with a specific user.
GetClaimByIdAsync	Fetch a specific claim by ID	Retrieve details of a specific claim using its unique identifier.
CreateNewClaimAsync	Create a new claim	Submit a new claim to the backend API.
UpdateClaimAsync	Update an existing claim	Modify the details of an existing claim.
UpdateClaimStatusAsync	Update the status of a claim	Change the status of a claim and optionally update the approved amount.
DeleteClaimAsync	Delete a specific claim by ID	Remove a specific claim from the backend API.

IClaimsManager.cs

```
using BenefitsManager.Backend.Bff.Api.Common;
using BenefitsManager.Backend.Bff.Api.Models;

namespace BenefitsManager.Backend.Bff.Api.Services
{
    public interface IClaimsManager
    {
        Task<List<ClaimModel>> GetClaimsByCreatorAsync(string userId);
```

```
        Task<ClaimModel?> GetClaimByIdAsync(Guid claimId);
        Task<Guid> CreateNewClaimAsync(string merchant, decimal
        claimedAmount, long purchaseDate, string categoryCode,
        string description, string receiptPath, UserModel
        createdBy);
        Task<bool> UpdateClaimAsync(Guid claimId, string
        merchant, decimal claimedAmount, long purchaseDate,
        string categoryCode, string description, string
        receiptPath);
        Task<bool> UpdateClaimStatusAsync(Guid claimId, decimal
        approvedAmount, ClaimStatus newStatus, string comment,
        UserModel setBy);
        Task<bool> DeleteClaimAsync(Guid claimId);
    }
}
```

FakeClaimsManager.cs

```
using System.Collections.Generic;
using System.Linq;
using BenefitsManager.Backend.Bff.Api.Common;
using BenefitsManager.Backend.Bff.Api.Models;

namespace BenefitsManager.Backend.Bff.Api.Services
{
    public class FakeClaimsManager : IClaimsManager
    {
        private readonly List<ClaimModel> _claimsList = new
        List<ClaimModel>();
        private readonly List<UserModel> _usersList = new
        List<UserModel>();
```

```csharp
private readonly List<ClaimCategoryModel> _
claimCategoriesList =
new List<ClaimCategoryModel>();

public FakeClaimsManager()
{
    GenerateRandomUsers();
    GenerateRandomCategories();
    GenerateRandomClaims();
}

private void GenerateRandomClaims()
{
    for (int i = 0; i < 10; i++)
    {
        var randomNo = Random.Shared.Next(1, 6);

        var claimId = Guid.NewGuid();

        var claim = new ClaimModel
        {
            ClaimId = claimId,
            Merchant = $"Merchant-{i}",
            ClaimedAmount = i * 10,
            PurchaseDate = DateTimeOffset.Now.AddDays
            (-randomNo).ToUnixTimeMilliseconds(),
            Category = _claimCategoriesList.First
            (c =>c.CategoryCode == $"CAT00{randomNo}"),
            Description = "Random description" + randomNo,
            StatusLog = new List<ClaimStatusModel>
            {
                new ClaimStatusModel
                {
```

CHAPTER 2   DEPLOYING FIRST CONTAINERIZED APP TO AZURE CONTAINER APPS

```
                    Status = ClaimStatus.Pending,
                    Comment = "", SetBy = _usersList.
                    First(u=>u.Email == $"user{randomNo}
                    @mail.com") , Ts = DateTimeOffset.
                    Now.AddHours(-randomNo).ToUnixTime
                    Milliseconds()
                }
            },
            CurrentStatus = ClaimStatus.Pending,
            ReceiptPath = $"https://storage.blob.core.
            windows.net/claims/{claimId}/receipt.pdf",
            CreatedBy = _usersList.First(u => u.Email
            == $"user{randomNo}@mail.com"),
            ApprovedAmount = null,
            CreatedOn = DateTimeOffset.Now.AddHours
            (-randomNo).ToUnixTimeMilliseconds(),
            ModifiedOn = null
        };

        _claimsList.Add(claim);
    }
}

private void GenerateRandomUsers()
{
    for (int i = 1; i < 6; i++)
    {
        var user = new UserModel
        {
            Id = Guid.NewGuid().ToString(),
            Email = $"user{i}@mail.com",
            Name = $"User-{i}"
        };
```

35

```csharp
            _usersList.Add(user);
        }
    }

    private void GenerateRandomCategories()
    {
        var categories = new List<ClaimCategoryModel>
        {
            new ClaimCategoryModel { CategoryCode = "CAT001",
            ParentCategoryName = "Clothing and shoes",
            CategoryName = "Athletic Accessories" },
            new ClaimCategoryModel { CategoryCode = "CAT002",
            ParentCategoryName = "Clothing and shoes",
            CategoryName = "Athletic Apparel" },
            new ClaimCategoryModel { CategoryCode = "CAT003",
            ParentCategoryName = "Fitness Activities",
            CategoryName = "Gym" },
            new ClaimCategoryModel { CategoryCode = "CAT004",
            ParentCategoryName = "Fitness Activities",
            CategoryName = "Fitness Classes" },
            new ClaimCategoryModel { CategoryCode = "CAT005",
            ParentCategoryName = "Home Office",
            CategoryName = "Desks
            and Chairs" }
        };

        _claimCategoriesList.AddRange(categories);

    }
    public Task<List<ClaimModel>>
    GetClaimsByCreatorAsync(string userId)
```

```csharp
{
    var claimsList = _claimsList.Where(t =>
    t.CreatedBy.Email.Equals(userId)).
    OrderByDescending(o =>
    o.CreatedOn).ToList();
    return Task.FromResult(claimsList);
}

public Task<ClaimModel?> GetClaimByIdAsync(Guid claimId)
{
    var claimModel = _claimsList.FirstOrDefault(t =>
    t.ClaimId.Equals(claimId));
    return Task.FromResult(claimModel);
}

public Task<Guid> CreateNewClaimAsync(string merchant,
                                      decimal claimedAmount,
                                      long purchaseDate,
                                      string categoryCode,
                                      string description,
                                      string receiptPath,
                                      UserModel createdBy)
{
    var claimModel = new ClaimModel()
    {
        ClaimId = Guid.NewGuid(),
```

CHAPTER 2   DEPLOYING FIRST CONTAINERIZED APP TO AZURE CONTAINER APPS

```
        Merchant = merchant,
        ClaimedAmount = claimedAmount,
        PurchaseDate = purchaseDate,
        Category = _claimCategoriesList.First(c =>
        c.CategoryCode == categoryCode),
        Description = description,
        StatusLog = new List<ClaimStatusModel>
    {
        new ClaimStatusModel
        {
            Status = ClaimStatus.Pending,
            Comment = "",
            SetBy = createdBy,
            Ts = DateTimeOffset.Now.
            ToUnixTimeMilliseconds()
        }
    },
        CurrentStatus = ClaimStatus.Pending,
        ReceiptPath = receiptPath,
        CreatedBy = createdBy,
        CreatedOn = DateTimeOffset.Now.
        ToUnixTimeMilliseconds(),
        ModifiedOn = null
    };

    _claimsList.Add(claimModel);

    return Task.FromResult(claimModel.ClaimId);
}

public Task<bool> UpdateClaimAsync(Guid claimId,
                                    string merchant,
```

CHAPTER 2   DEPLOYING FIRST CONTAINERIZED APP TO AZURE CONTAINER APPS

```
                                    decimal
                                    claimedAmount,
                                    long purchaseDate,
                                    string
                                    categoryCode,
                                    string description,
                                    string receiptPath)
{
    var claimModel = _claimsList.FirstOrDefault(t =>
    t.ClaimId.Equals(claimId));

    if (claimModel == null)
    {
        return Task.FromResult(false);
    }

    claimModel.Merchant = merchant;
    claimModel.ClaimedAmount = claimedAmount;
    claimModel.PurchaseDate = purchaseDate;
    claimModel.Category = _claimCategoriesList.
    First(c => c.CategoryCode == categoryCode);
    claimModel.Description = description;
    claimModel.ReceiptPath = receiptPath;
    claimModel.ModifiedOn =
    DateTimeOffset.Now.ToUnixTimeMilliseconds();

    return Task.FromResult(true);
}

public Task<bool> UpdateClaimStatusAsync(Guid claimId,
                                    decimal
                                    approvedAmount,
                                    ClaimStatus
                                    newStatus,
```

39

```csharp
                                    string comment,
                                    UserModel setBy)
{
    var claimModel = _claimsList.FirstOrDefault(t =>
    t.ClaimId.Equals(claimId));

    if (claimModel == null)
    {
        return Task.FromResult(false);
    }

    claimModel.ApprovedAmount = approvedAmount;

    claimModel.StatusLog.Add(new ClaimStatusModel
    {
        Status = newStatus,
        Comment = comment,
        SetBy = setBy,
        Ts = DateTimeOffset.Now.ToUnixTimeMilli
        seconds()
    });

    claimModel.CurrentStatus = newStatus;
    claimModel.ModifiedOn =
    DateTimeOffset.Now.ToUnixTimeMilliseconds();

    return Task.FromResult(true);
}

public Task<bool> DeleteClaimAsync(Guid claimId)
{
    var claimModel = _claimsList.FirstOrDefault(t =>
    t.ClaimId.Equals(claimId) && t.CurrentStatus ==
    ClaimStatus.Pending);
```

```
            if (claimModel == null)
            {
                return Task.FromResult(false);
            }

            _claimsList.Remove(claimModel);

            return Task.FromResult(true);
        }
    }
}
```

2.4.4 Program Configuration

The Program.cs file sets up the ASP.NET application, configures services, and defines HTTP endpoints for the API.

```
using System.Security.Claims;
using BenefitsManager.Backend.Bff.Api.Models;
using BenefitsManager.Backend.Bff.Api.Services;
using Microsoft.AspNetCore.Http.HttpResults;
using Microsoft.AspNetCore.Mvc;

var builder = WebApplication.CreateBuilder(args);

// Add services to the container.
builder.Services.AddSingleton<IClaimsManager,
FakeClaimsManager>();
builder.Services.AddOpenApi();

var app = builder.Build();

// Configure the HTTP request pipeline.
if (app.Environment.IsDevelopment())
{
```

CHAPTER 2   DEPLOYING FIRST CONTAINERIZED APP TO AZURE CONTAINER APPS

```
    app.MapOpenApi();
}

app.UseHttpsRedirection();

// Define the API endpoints
app.MapGet("/api/claims", async ([FromQuery(Name = "userId")]
string userId, IClaimsManager claimsManager) =>
    TypedResults.Ok(await claimsManager.GetClaimsByCreatorAsync
    (userId)))
    .WithName("GetClaimsByCreator")
    .Produces<List<ClaimModel>>();

app.MapPost("/api/claims", async ([FromBody] ClaimAddModel
claimModel, IClaimsManager claimsManager) =>
{
    var claimId = await claimsManager.CreateNewClaimAsync
    (claimModel.Merchant,
                claimModel.ClaimedAmount,
                claimModel.PurchaseDate,
                claimModel.CategoryCode,
                claimModel.Description,
                claimModel.ReceiptPath,
                claimModel.CreatedBy);

    return Results.Created($"/api/claims/{claimId}", claimId);
}).WithName("CreateNewClaim")
    .Produces<Created<Guid>>();

app.MapPut("/api/claims/{claimId}", async ([FromRoute] Guid
claimId, [FromBody] ClaimUpdateModel claimModel, IClaimsManager
claimsManager) =>
    await claimsManager.UpdateClaimAsync(claimId,
    claimModel.Merchant,
```

```
        claimModel.ClaimedAmount,
        claimModel.PurchaseDate,
        claimModel.CategoryCode,
        claimModel.Description,
        claimModel.ReceiptPath)
        is bool updateResult ? Results.Ok(updateResult) : Results.
        NotFound()
    ).WithName("UpdateClaim")
     .Produces<Ok<bool>>()
     .Produces<NotFound>();

app.MapPut("/api/claims/{claimId}/status", async
([FromRoute] Guid claimId, [FromBody] ClaimStatusUpdateModel
claimStatusUpdateModel, IClaimsManager claimsManager) =>
        await claimsManager.UpdateClaimStatusAsync(claimId,
        claimStatusUpdateModel.ApprovedAmount,
        claimStatusUpdateModel.NewStatus,
        claimStatusUpdateModel.Comment,
        claimStatusUpdateModel.SetBy)
        is bool updateResult ? Results.Ok(updateResult) : Results.
        NotFound()
    ).WithName("UpdateClaimStatus")
     .Produces<Ok<bool>>()
     .Produces<NotFound>();

app.MapDelete("/api/claims/{claimId}", async ([FromRoute] Guid
claimId, IClaimsManager claimsManager) =>
        await claimsManager.DeleteClaimAsync(claimId)
        ? Results.Ok() : Results.NotFound()
    ).WithName("DeleteClaim")
     .Produces<Ok>()
     .Produces<NotFound>();

app.Run();
```

2.4.5 Docker Configuration

To deploy the BenefitsClaimManager.Backend API to Azure Container Apps, we need to containerize this application and push the container image to Azure Container Registry.

You can use Visual Studio or Visual Studio Code to add Docker file support. In this section, we will see both ways; however, going forward, we will use only Visual Studio Code.

Using Visual Studio

Right-click on the *BenefitsManager.Backend.Bff.Api* project and select **Add Docker support**. The Container Scaffolding options popup will open as shown in Figure 2-2. Select the following options:

- Choose Linux when prompted to choose the operating system.

- Choose Dockerfile for container build type.

- Choose Default (9.0) value for container image distro.

- Select the Front-end project from the drop-down for the Docker build context section.

- Dockerfile and .dockerignore files are added to the workspace.

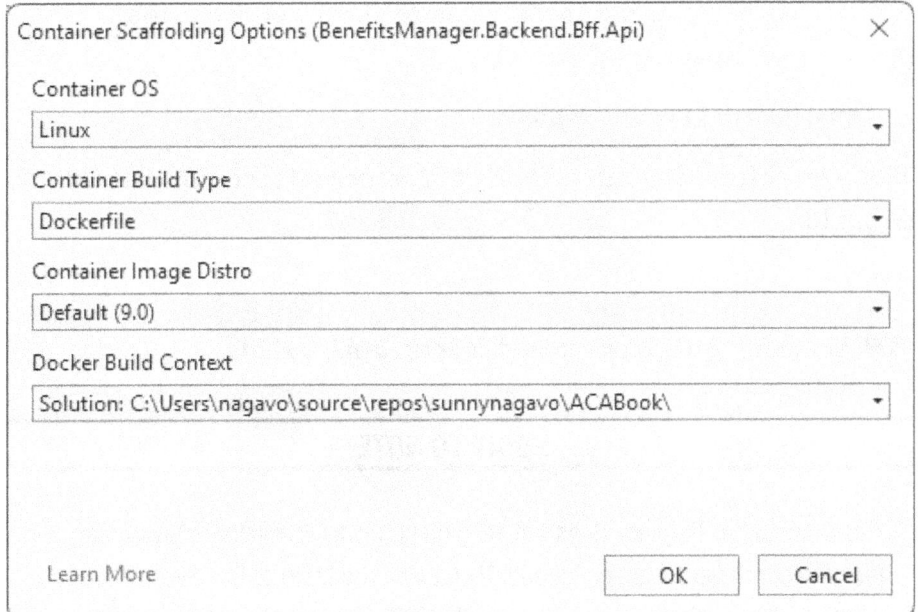

Figure 2-2. *Container Scaffolding Options popup to add Docker file support*

Using Visual Studio Code

Open the VS Code Command Palette (Ctrl+Shift+P) and select Docker: Add Docker Files to Workspace.

- Use .NET:ASP.NET Core when prompted for the application platform.

- Choose the newly created project, if prompted.

- Choose Linux when prompted to choose the operating system.

- Set the application port to 5000. This is arbitrary but memorable for this workshop.

- You will be asked if you want to add Docker Compose files. Select No.

- Dockerfile and .dockerignore files are added to the workspace.

Open Dockerfile and replace

```
FROM --platform=$BUILDPLATFORM mcr.microsoft.com/dotnet/sdk:9.0 AS build
```

with

```
FROM mcr.microsoft.com/dotnet/sdk:9.0 AS build
```

> **POINT TO NOTE**
>
> Azure Container Registry does not set $BUILDPLATFORM presently when building containers. This consequently causes the build to fail. See https://github.com/microsoft/vscode-docker/issues/4149 for details. Therefore, we removed it from the file as a workaround mentioned by the product team.

Finally, we have the Dockerfile that defines how to build and run the application in a container.

```
FROM mcr.microsoft.com/dotnet/aspnet:9.0-preview AS base
WORKDIR /app
EXPOSE 5000

ENV ASPNETCORE_URLS=http://+:5000

USER app
FROM mcr.microsoft.com/dotnet/sdk:9.0-preview AS build
ARG configuration=Release
WORKDIR /src
COPY ["BenefitsManager.Backend.Bff.Api/BenefitsManager.Backend.Bff.Api.csproj", "BenefitsManager.Backend.Bff.Api/"]
```

```
RUN dotnet restore "BenefitsManager.Backend.Bff.Api/
BenefitsManager.Backend.Bff.Api.csproj"
COPY . .
WORKDIR "/src/BenefitsManager.Backend.Bff.Api"
RUN dotnet build "BenefitsManager.Backend.Bff.Api.csproj" -c
$configuration -o /app/build

FROM build AS publish
ARG configuration=Release
RUN dotnet publish "BenefitsManager.Backend.Bff.Api.csproj" -c
$configuration -o /app/publish /p:UseAppHost=false

FROM base AS final
WORKDIR /app
COPY --from=publish /app/publish .
ENTRYPOINT ["dotnet", "BenefitsManager.Backend.Bff.Api.dll"]
```

2.5 Use .http Files in Visual Studio to Validate API

The Visual Studio team has added .http file editor support, which is a convenient way to test ASP.NET API projects by sending HTTP requests directly within the IDE without needing external tools like Postman or curl. A file can contain multiple requests by using lines with ### as delimiters. The example below shows a GET request to the api/claims endpoint by passing a specific user id in the query string.

```
@BenefitsManager.Backend.Bff.Api_HostAddress = http://
localhost:5103

GET {{BenefitsManager.Backend.Bff.Api_HostAddress}}/api/
claims/?userId=user3@mail.com
```

Accept: application/json

###

Clicking Send request will make an http request, and the response is returned as JSON within a side pane as shown in Figure 2-3.

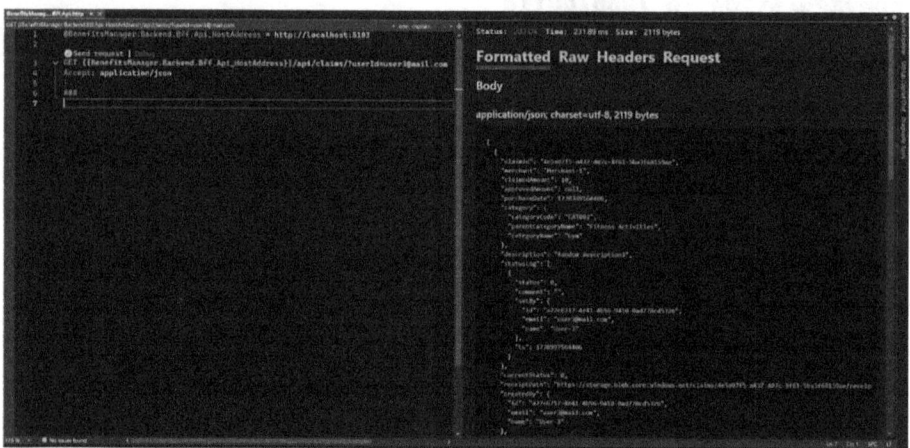

Figure 2-3. *Receiving JSON response by sending a request from the .http file*

2.6 Deploying to Azure Container Apps

Now that we understand the code base, we can deploy the application to Azure Container Apps, but before that, we need to set up the underlying infrastructure like Azure Container Registry to store images, Azure Container Apps environment, Networking Infrastructure, Log Analytics, and Application Insights.

2.6.1 Create Azure Infrastructure

We will be using **Azure CLI** to deploy the Web API Backend to ACA. First, we need to ensure that our CLI is updated. Then we log in to Azure.

CHAPTER 2 DEPLOYING FIRST CONTAINERIZED APP TO AZURE CONTAINER APPS

```
# Upgrade the Azure CLI
az upgrade

# Install/upgrade the Azure Container Apps & Application
Insights extensions
az extension add --upgrade --name containerapp
az extension add --upgrade --name application-insights

# Log in to Azure
az login
```

You may be able to use the queried Azure subscription ID, or you may need to set it manually depending on your setup.

```
# Retrieve the currently active Azure subscription ID
$AZURE_SUBSCRIPTION_ID = az account show --query id
--output tsv

# Set a specific Azure Subscription ID (if you have multiple
subscriptions)
# $AZURE_SUBSCRIPTION_ID = "<Your Azure Subscription ID>"
# Your Azure Subscription id which you can find on the
Azure portal
az account set --subscription $AZURE_SUBSCRIPTION_ID

echo $AZURE_SUBSCRIPTION_ID
```

Execute the variables below in the PowerShell console to use them inside Chapters 2 and 3. Some of these variables must be globally unique, which we attempt by creating $RANDOM_STRING.

```
# Create a random, 4-digit, Azure safe string
$RANDOM_STRING=-join ((97..122) + (48..57) | Get-Random -Count 4
| ForEach-Object { [char]$_ })

$RESOURCE_GROUP="rg-benefits-manager"
```

```
$LOCATION="eastus"
$ENVIRONMENT="cae-benefits-manager"
$WORKSPACE_NAME="log-benefits-manager-$RANDOM_STRING"
$APPINSIGHTS_NAME="appi-benefits-manager-$RANDOM_STRING"
$BE_BFF_API_NAME="ca-benefitsmanager-bff-api"
$AZURE_CONTAINER_REGISTRY_
NAME="crbenefitsmanager$RANDOM_STRING"
$TARGET_PORT=5000
```

Create a resource group to organize the services related to the application; run the below command:

```
az group create `
--name $RESOURCE_GROUP `
--location "$LOCATION"
```

2.6.2 Create Log Analytics Workspace and Application Insights

Create an Azure Log Analytics workspace that will provide a common place to store the system and application log data from all container apps running in the environment. Each environment should have its own Log Analytics workspace.

```
# Create the Log Analytics workspace
az monitor log-analytics workspace create `
--resource-group $RESOURCE_GROUP `
--workspace-name $WORKSPACE_NAME

# Retrieve the Log Analytics workspace ID
$WORKSPACE_ID=az monitor log-analytics workspace show `
--resource-group $RESOURCE_GROUP `
--workspace-name $WORKSPACE_NAME `
```

```
--query customerId `
--output tsv

# Retrieve the Log Analytics workspace secret
$WORKSPACE_SECRET=az monitor log-analytics workspace get-shared-keys `
--resource-group $RESOURCE_GROUP `
--workspace-name $WORKSPACE_NAME `
--query primarySharedKey `
--output tsv
```

Create an Application Insights instance that will be used mainly for distributed tracing between different container apps within the ACA environment to provide searching for and visualizing an end-to-end flow of a given execution or transaction. To create it, run the command below:

```
# Create Application Insights instance
az monitor app-insights component create `
--resource-group $RESOURCE_GROUP `
--location $LOCATION `
--app $APPINSIGHTS_NAME `
--workspace $WORKSPACE_NAME

# Get Application Insights Instrumentation Key
$APPINSIGHTS_INSTRUMENTATIONKEY=($(az monitor app-insights component show `
--resource-group $RESOURCE_GROUP `
--app $APPINSIGHTS_NAME ) | ConvertFrom-Json).instrumentationKey
```

2.6.3 Azure Container Infrastructure

Create an Azure Container Registry (ACR) instance in the resource group to store images of all microservices we are going to build throughout this book. Make sure that you set the admin-enabled flag to true in order to seamlessly authenticate the Azure container app when trying to create the container app using the image stored in ACR.

```
az acr create `
--name $AZURE_CONTAINER_REGISTRY_NAME `
--resource-group $RESOURCE_GROUP `
--sku Basic `
--admin-enabled true
```

Now we will create an Azure Container Apps environment. The ACA environment acts as a secure boundary around a group of container apps that we are going to provide. Refer to Chapter 1 for more details about the ACA environment.

```
# Create the ACA environment
az containerapp env create `
--name $ENVIRONMENT `
--resource-group $RESOURCE_GROUP `
--location $LOCATION `
--logs-workspace-id $WORKSPACE_ID `
--logs-workspace-key $WORKSPACE_SECRET `
--dapr-instrumentation-key $APPINSIGHTS_INSTRUMENTATIONKEY
```

2.6.4 Build and Publish the Docker Image

Build the *BenefitsManager.Backend.Bff.Api* project on Azure Container Registry (ACR) and push the Docker image to ACR. Use the below command to initiate the image build and push process using ACR. The

"." at the end of the command represents the Docker build context; in our case, we need to be in the parent directory that hosts the .csproj.

```
az acr build `
--registry $AZURE_CONTAINER_REGISTRY_NAME `
--image "benefitsmanager/$BE_BFF_API_NAME" `
--file 'BenefitsManager.Backend.Bff.Api/Dockerfile' .
```

Once this step is completed, you can verify the results by going to the Azure portal and checking that a new repository named **"benefitsmanager/ca-benefitsmanager-bff-api"** has been created and that there is a new Docker image with a latest tag as shown in Figure 2-4.

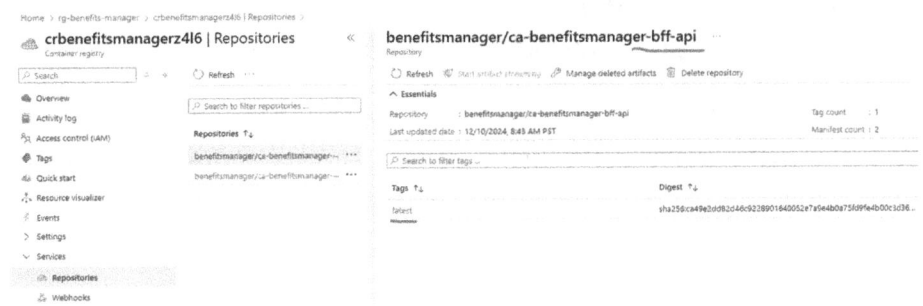

Figure 2-4. *ACR repository containing the latest Docker image*

2.6.5 Deploy to Azure Container Apps

The last step here is to create and deploy the API to ACA by running the below command:

```
$fqdn=(az containerapp create `
--name $BE_BFF_API_NAME `
--resource-group $RESOURCE_GROUP `
--environment $ENVIRONMENT `
--image "$AZURE_CONTAINER_REGISTRY_NAME.azurecr.io/
benefitsmanager/$BE_BFF_API_NAME" `
```

CHAPTER 2 DEPLOYING FIRST CONTAINERIZED APP TO AZURE CONTAINER APPS

```
--registry-server "$AZURE_CONTAINER_REGISTRY_NAME.azurecr.io" `
--target-port $TARGET_PORT `
--ingress 'external' `
--min-replicas 1 `
--max-replicas 1 `
--cpu 0.25 `
--memory 0.5Gi `
--query properties.configuration.ingress.fqdn `
--output tsv)

$BE_BFF_API_EXTERNAL_BASE_URL="https://$fqdn"

echo "See a listing of claims created by user3:"
echo "https://$fqdn/api/claims/?userId=user3@mail.com"
```

Once this step is completed, you can now verify the deployment of the first ACA by navigating to the Azure portal and selecting the resource group named *"rg-benefits-manager"*. You should see the five resources selected in Figure 2-5.

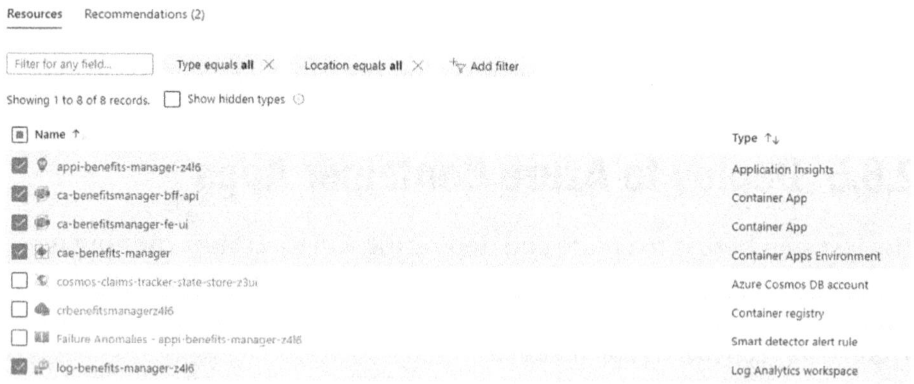

Figure 2-5. *List of resources created inside the resource group*

2.7 Accessing Published API

We can use Fiddler or Postman to invoke the deployed API to retrieve the claims. You can get the application URL by navigating to the deployed Azure container app on the Azure portal overview tab. Navigating to the URL in the browser by passing user id as query string, you will get a list of claims as shown in Figure 2-6.

Figure 2-6. List of claims returned for a specific user id

2.8 Summary

In this chapter, we set up a development environment, created the first microservice using ASP.NET Minimal APIs, and containerized it using Docker. We pushed this container image to Azure Container Registry (ACR) and deployed it to Azure Container Apps (ACA). You learned about how to use ACR to store and manage container images and explored key configurations required for ACA deployments. With this foundation, you are now ready to explore additional Azure services to build a robust cloud-native application.

In Chapter 3, we will explore leveraging Blazor Web framework to create frontend web applications to consume these APIs.

CHAPTER 3

Creating and Deploying Frontend – Blazor Web Application

In Chapter 2, we looked at creating and deploying the Benefits Manager backend API to Azure Container Apps. In this chapter, you will be introduced to the frontend web application, specifically its functionality. We will leverage Blazor framework to create the frontend portal which will interact with the backend APIs. The learning objectives for this chapter include the following:

- Introduction to Blazor framework.

- Create Blazor project *"BenefitsManager.Frontend. WebPortal.Ui"* – which acts as the frontend for our Benefits Manager application.

- Explore various tools and technology options used to build the UI.

- Create the underlying Azure infrastructure.

CHAPTER 3   CREATING AND DEPLOYING FRONTEND – BLAZOR WEB APPLICATION

- Deploy the frontend to ACA and invoke the backend APIs from Chapter 2.
- Update the backend Web API container app Ingress property to restrict traffic.

3.1 Setting Up a Development Environment

Make sure you have your development environment set up and configured by installing or setting up the resources below:

- An Azure account with an active subscription – https://azure.microsoft.com/free/?ref=microsoft.com&utm_source=microsoft.com&utm_medium=docs&utm_campaign=visualstudio.

- Dotnet 9.0 or a higher version – https://dotnet.microsoft.com/en-us/download.

- PowerShell 7.0 or a higher version (for Windows users only) – https://learn.microsoft.com/en-us/powershell/scripting/install/installing-powershell-on-windows?view=powershell-7.4#installing-the-msi-package.

- Docker Desktop – https://docs.docker.com/desktop/install/windows-install/.

- Latest Visual Studio – https://visualstudio.microsoft.com/vs/.

- Install the latest version of Visual Studio with the **ASP.NET and web development workload** to get Blazor templates.

- Azure CLI – https://docs.microsoft.com/cli/azure/install-azure-cli.

3.2 Introduction to Blazor Framework

Blazor is a modern frontend web framework based on HTML, CSS, and C# that helps us in building web applications faster. Blazor has emerged as a powerful tool in recent times for creating interactive web applications. Integrating C# with web development, Blazor offers a different approach in creating dynamic and user-engaging experiences. For more details, please refer to Microsoft's official learn documentation: https://learn.microsoft.com/en-us/aspnet/core/blazor/?view=aspnetcore-8.0.

POINT TO NOTE

This chapter expects readers to have some understanding of Blazor framework. If you have never used Blazor, I also highly recommend the book *Microsoft Blazor* from Apress, which will help you in getting started with Blazor framework: https://link.springer.com/book/10.1007/978-1-4842-7845-1.

3.3 Why Blazor for Frontend?

Blazor, a revolutionary framework within the .NET ecosystem, offers a compelling set of advantages that make it a powerful tool for modern web development. Let's explore some of the key benefits that Blazor brings to the table:

1. **Rapid Web UI Development with Reusable Components**

   Blazor's component-based architecture empowers developers to create reusable UI elements that can be easily combined to build complex applications.

This modular approach promotes code reusability, accelerates development, and enhances code maintainability.

2. **Rich Interactivity with C#**

   One of Blazor's standout features is its ability to handle arbitrary UI events from the browser and implement component logic entirely in C#. This eliminates the need for complex JavaScript-based event handling, providing a more streamlined and intuitive development experience.

3. **Unified Development Stack**

   Blazor gives developers an all-in-one stack to build their whole web app, from front to back using just one language and framework. This cuts down on switching between contexts, helps share code better, and creates a more unified development setting.

4. **Efficient Rendering with Diff-Based Techniques**

   Blazor's smart change-based rendering system makes sure the needed parts of the DOM get updates when changes happen. This cuts down on extra rendering and helps create a smoother and quicker user experience.

5. **Flexible Deployment Options**

   Blazor lets developers pick between server-side and client-side rendering. This allows you to choose the deployment model that works best for your app's needs, making sure it runs well and can grow as needed.

6. **Server-Rendered Apps**

    Blazor has built-in support to improve server-rendered web apps bit by bit. This makes sure users with older browsers or slow Internet connections still have a smooth experience.

7. **Interoperability with JavaScript**

    While Blazor tries to use less JavaScript, it doesn't get rid of it. Blazor works with JavaScript libraries and browser APIs, so you can still use all the great JavaScript tools and frameworks out there.

8. **Integration with Existing Applications**

    Blazor can be integrated with existing MVC, Razor Pages, or JavaScript-based applications. This flexibility enables you to gradually adopt Blazor into your existing projects without having to redo everything.

9. **Powerful Tooling Support**

    Both Visual Studio and Visual Studio Code support Blazor, giving developers a lot of helpful tools and features to make their work easier. From finishing your code for you and finding bugs to designing parts and testing, Blazor's tools offer everything you need to develop your app.

10. **Cross-Platform Development**

    Blazor doesn't stop at web apps. You can also use it to build native mobile and desktop applications with Blazor Hybrid. This lets you create user experiences that look and feel the same across different platforms while using the Blazor skills you already have.

Blazor's mix of these features makes it a great choice for modern web development. By leveraging Blazor's capabilities, developers can build high-performance, interactive, and scalable web applications with ease.

3.4 Create Frontend Web App Project

You can use Visual Studio UI or CLI to create and initialize web projects.

Using CLI

Open the VS developer command prompt and go to the root folder of the previously created solution from Chapter 2 and run the command below:

```
dotnet new blazorserver -o BenefitsManager.Frontend.WebPortal.Ui
```

This command will initialize and create an ASP.NET Blazor web app project. To add this newly created project to the existing solution, run the below command:

```
dotnet sln add BenefitsManager.Frontend.WebPortal.Ui/BenefitsManager.Frontend.WebPortal.Ui.csproj
```

Using Visual Studio

Open the Benefits Manager solution from Visual Studio or VS Code editor. Right-click on the solution, click Add – New Project to select "Blazor Web App" from the list of templates as shown in Figure 3-1. Delete weather-related boilerplate code, which was added by default by the template.

CHAPTER 3   CREATING AND DEPLOYING FRONTEND – BLAZOR WEB APPLICATION

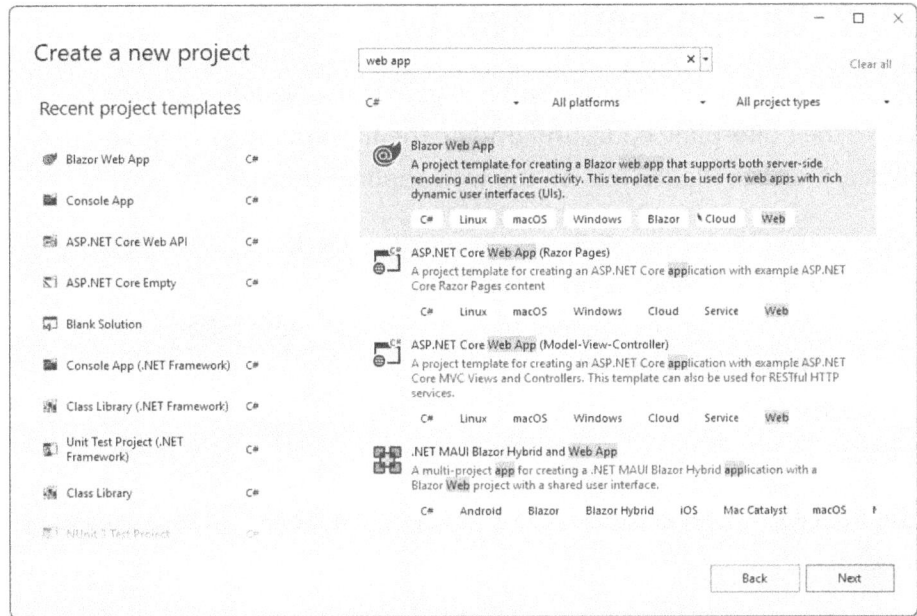

Figure 3-1. *List of available Blazor project templates inside Visual Studio 2022*

3.5 Understanding the Code Structure

3.5.1 ClaimModel.cs Class

Open the Models folder inside the Frontend project, and add a new file called **ClaimModel.cs**. Copy the contents from the **ClaimModel.cs** file in the Backend project, which was created in Chapter 2. In the upcoming chapters, we will create a common library and move these common classes to be shared across projects without duplicating code.

3.5.2 Components Layout

Open the Components folder and navigate to the **NavMenu.razor** file, delete the boilerplate code, and update the file contents as shown below to display Manage Claims text on the web application.

```
<div class="top-row ps-3 navbar navbar-dark">
    <div class="container-fluid">
        <a class="navbar-brand" href="">BenefitsManager.
        Frontend.WebPortal.Ui</a>
    </div>
</div>

<input type="checkbox" title="Navigation menu" class="navbar-toggler" />

<div class="nav-scrollable" onclick="document.querySelector('.navbar-toggler').click()">
    <nav class="flex-column">
        <div class="nav-item px-3">
            <NavLink class="nav-link" href=""
            Match="NavLinkMatch.All">
                <span class="bi bi-house-door-fill-nav-menu"
                aria-hidden="true"></span> Manage Claims
            </NavLink>
        </div>
    </nav>
</div>
```

3.5.3 ClaimsService.cs

In order to interact with the backend services to retrieve data, we need the ClaimsService class, which is a key component in the BenefitsManager. Frontend.WebPortal.Ui project, created to handle HTTP requests related to claims. Its main usage is to provide a centralized service to facilitate communication between the frontend and the backend API.

Right-click on the "BenefitsManager.Frontend.WebPortal.Ui" project and select "Add new folder"; name it as **Services**. Under the **Services** folder, add a new file called **ClaimsService.cs**. The ClaimsService class encapsulates the logic for interacting with the backend API to manage claims. It provides methods to create, read, update, and delete claims, making it a critical component for the frontend application to handle claim-related operations efficiently. A detailed list of methods is shown in Table 3-1.

Table 3-1. *List of operations/methods inside the ClaimsService.cs class*

Operation	Use Case	Purpose	Implementation
GetClaimsAsync	Fetch all claims for a specific user	Retrieve a list of claims associated with a specific user.	Sends a GET request to api/claims/?{userId=<userid>}. Returns an empty list if no claims are found for that particular userid
GetClaimByIdAsync	Fetch a specific claim by ID	Retrieve details of a specific claim using its unique identifier.	Sends a GET request to api/claims/{claimId}. Throws InvalidOperationException if claim not found

(*continued*)

CHAPTER 3 CREATING AND DEPLOYING FRONTEND – BLAZOR WEB APPLICATION

Table 3-1. (*continued*)

Operation	Use Case	Purpose	Implementation
CreateClaimAsync	Create a new claim	Submit a new claim to the backend API.	Sends a POST request to api/claims with the claim data in the request body
UpdateClaimAsync	Update an existing claim	Modify the details of an existing claim.	Sends a PUT request to api/claims/{claim.ClaimId} with the updated claim data
DeleteClaimAsync	Delete a specific claim by ID	Remove a specific claim from the backend API.	Sends a DELETE request to api/claims/{id}

In this chapter, we will leverage the *HttpClient* class to make direct calls to the locally running backend service. By using HttpClient and asynchronous programming, it ensures that the application remains responsive while performing these operations.

By adding all the methods, the ***ClaimsService.cs*** class will look exactly as this code:

```
using BenefitsManager.Frontend.WebPortal.Ui.Models;
namespace BenefitsManager.Frontend.WebPortal.Ui.Services
{
    public class ClaimsService
    {
        private readonly HttpClient _httpClient;
        public ClaimsService(HttpClient httpClient)
        {
            _httpClient = httpClient;
        }
```

CHAPTER 3   CREATING AND DEPLOYING FRONTEND – BLAZOR WEB APPLICATION

```
public async Task<List<ClaimModel>> GetClaimsAsync()
{
    var claims = await _httpClient.GetFromJsonAsync
    <List<ClaimModel>>("api/claims/?userId=user3@
    mail.com");
    if (claims == null)
    {
        return new List<ClaimModel>();
    }
    return claims;
}

public async Task<ClaimModel> GetClaimByIdAsync
(Guid claimId)
{
    var claim = await _httpClient.GetFromJsonAsync
    <ClaimModel>($"api/claims/{claimId}");
    if (claim == null)
    {
        throw new InvalidOperationException("Claim not
        found.");
    }
    return claim;
}

public async Task<HttpResponseMessage>
CreateClaimAsync(ClaimAddModel claim)
{
    return await _httpClient.PostAsJsonAsync("api/
    claims", claim);
}
```

```csharp
    public async Task UpdateClaimAsync(ClaimModel claim)
    {
        await _httpClient.PutAsJsonAsync($"api/claims/
        {claim.ClaimId}", claim);
    }
    public async Task DeleteClaimAsync(Guid id)
    {
        await _httpClient.DeleteAsync($"api/claims/{id}");
    }
  }
}
```

3.5.4 Blazor Components

The components in the Pages folder of the *BenefitsManager.Frontend. WebPortal.Ui* project provide UI for managing claims. Here is the list of components that serve a specific purpose:

- **NewClaim.razor:** Provides a form for creating a new claim

- **ClaimDetails.razor:** Displays detailed information about a specific claim

- **Home.razor:** Home page that displays a list of claims and provides options to view details, create new claims, and delete existing claims

NewClaim.razor
The NewClaim.razor component provides a user-friendly interface for creating new claims. It leverages Blazor's data binding and event handling to capture user inputs such as merchant information, claim amount, purchase date, category, and description. Once the form is filled out,

CHAPTER 3   CREATING AND DEPLOYING FRONTEND – BLAZOR WEB APPLICATION

the user can submit the claim, which will be sent to the backend API for processing. For easy understanding, let's split the file into multiple sections to understand the code better.

a. **Namespaces and Dependencies**

```
<!-- Client/Pages/NewClaim.razor →
@page "/new-claim"
@using BenefitsManager.Frontend.WebPortal.Ui.Models
@using BenefitsManager.Frontend.WebPortal.Ui.Services
@inject NavigationManager Navigation
@inject ClaimsService ClaimsService
```

Let's investigate different tags from the above code:

- @page: Defines the route for this component as /new-claim

- @using: Imports necessary namespaces, including models and services

- @inject: Injects the NavigationManager and ClaimsService for navigation and service operations

b. **User Interface**

```
<h3>Create New Claim</h3>

<div class="form-group">
    <label>Merchant</label>
    <input type="text" class="form-control"
    @bind="newClaim.Merchant" />
</div>
```

```
<div class="form-group">
    <label>Claimed Amount</label>
    <input type="number" class="form-control"
    @bind="newClaim.ClaimedAmount" />
</div>

<div class="form-group">
    <label>Purchase Date</label>
    <input type="date" class="form-control"
    @bind="purchaseDate" />
</div>

<div class="form-group">
    <label>Category</label>
    <select class="form-control" @bind="newClaim.
    CategoryCode">
        <option value="CAT001">Clothing and shoes |
        Athletic Accessories</option>
        <option value="CAT002">Clothing and shoes |
        Athletic Apparel</option>
        <option value="CAT003">Fitness Activities |
        Gym</option>
        <option value="CAT004">Fitness Activities |
        Fitness Classes</option>
        <option value="CAT005">Home Office | Desks and
        Chairs</option>
    </select>
</div>

<div class="form-group">
    <label>Description</label>
```

```
<textarea class="form-control" @bind="newClaim.
Description"></textarea>
</div>

<button class="btn btn-primary"
@onclick="SubmitNewClaim">Submit Claim</button>
```

This section of code includes input fields for filling out mandatory information to create a new claim. A button to submit the form is added at the end, which triggers the **SubmitNewClaim** method.

c. **Code Behind**

```
@code {
    private ClaimAddModel newClaim = new
    ClaimAddModel();
    private DateTime purchaseDate = DateTime.Today;
    // Default purchase date

    private async Task SubmitNewClaim()
    {
        // Convert purchaseDate to epoch timestamp
           (milliseconds since 1970-01-01)
        newClaim.PurchaseDate = new DateTimeOffset
        (purchaseDate).ToUnixTimeMilliseconds();
        newClaim.CreatedBy = new UserModel
        {
            Id = "2c5aa106-adce-4112-9a56-
            d37477ef18bf",
            Email = "user3@mail.com",
            Name = "User 3"
        };
```

```
            newClaim.ReceiptPath = "https://www.example.
            com/receipts/claim1.pdf";

            var response = await ClaimsService.
            CreateClaimAsync(newClaim);

            if (response.IsSuccessStatusCode)
            {
                Navigation.NavigateTo("/");
                // Redirect to homepage or another page
            }
            else
            {
                // Handle errors (display a message, log
                    the error, etc.)
                Console.WriteLine("Error submitting
                claim.");
            }
        }
    }
```

Note For simplicity, we hard-coded User 3 details when submitting new claims, which will be updated in upcoming chapters to retrieve logged-in user details.

Home.razor

The Home.razor component provides a user interface for managing claims. It allows logged-in users to view a list of recent claims with the option to navigate to the claims creation page, view details of a specific claim, and delete claims.

CHAPTER 3   CREATING AND DEPLOYING FRONTEND – BLAZOR WEB APPLICATION

Open the pages subfolder inside the components folder and delete **weather.razor** and **counter.razor** pages, which were added as boilerplate code from the initial Blazor template. Update the **Home.razor** file to display managed claims by invoking **ClaimsService** created in the above section. Navigating to the home page on the web browser will display a "Loading..." message till it retrieves data from the backend API service to display the list of claims.

We inject "**ClaimsService**" into the **Home.razor** file, which helps us in calling backend APIs. Update the **Home.Razor** file to look exactly as below.

Note   To avoid duplication, we won't discuss individual sections; however, all the razor files have similar format (namespace dependencies on the top, HTML section, code behind section).

```
<!-- Client/Pages/Claims.razor -->
@page "/"
@using BenefitsManager.Frontend.WebPortal.Ui.Models
@using BenefitsManager.Frontend.WebPortal.Ui.Services
@inject ClaimsService ClaimsService
@inject NavigationManager Navigation

<PageTitle>Manage Claims</PageTitle>

<h1>View recent claims</h1>

<hr>

@if (claims == null)
{
    <p><em>Loading...</em></p>
}
```

CHAPTER 3 CREATING AND DEPLOYING FRONTEND – BLAZOR WEB APPLICATION

```
else
{
    <div>
        <button class="btn btn-primary" @onclick="() =>
        NavigateToNewClaim()">New Claim</button>
    </div>
    <table class="table">
        <thead>
            <tr>
                <td>Merchant</td>
                <td>Receipt Date</td>
                <td>Amount</td>
                <td>Category</td>
                <td>Status</td>
                <td>Submit Date</td>
                <th>Actions</th>
            </tr>
        </thead>
        <tbody>
            @foreach (var claim in claims)
            {
                <tr>
                    <td>@claim.Merchant</td>
                    <td>@DateTimeOffset.FromUnixTimeMilli
                    seconds(claim.PurchaseDate).ToLocalTime().
                    ToString("yyyy-MM-dd HH:mm:ss")</td>
                    <td>@claim.ClaimedAmount</td>
                    <td>@claim.Category.CategoryName</td>
                    <td>@claim.CurrentStatus.ToString()</td>
                    <td>@DateTimeOffset.FromUnixTimeMilli
                    seconds(claim.CreatedOn).ToLocalTime().
                    ToString("yyyy-MM-dd HH:mm:ss")</td>
```

CHAPTER 3   CREATING AND DEPLOYING FRONTEND – BLAZOR WEB APPLICATION

```
                <td>
                    <button @onclick="() => GoToClaim
                    Details(claim.ClaimId.ToString())">View
                    Claim</button>
                    @* @((MarkupString)$"<a href='/claim/
                    {claim.ClaimId.ToString()}'>View
                    Claim</a>") *@
                </td>
            </tr>
        }
    </tbody>
</table>
}

@code {
    private List<ClaimModel> claims;

    protected override async Task OnInitializedAsync()
    {
        claims = await ClaimsService.GetClaimsAsync();
    }

     private void NavigateToNewClaim()
    {
        Navigation.NavigateTo("/new-claim");
    }

    private void GoToClaimDetails(string claimId)
    {
        string url = $"/claim/{claimId}";
        Console.WriteLine($"Navigating to: {url}");
        Navigation.NavigateTo(url);
    }
```

75

CHAPTER 3   CREATING AND DEPLOYING FRONTEND – BLAZOR WEB APPLICATION

```
    private async Task DeleteClaim(Guid id)
    {
        await ClaimsService.DeleteClaimAsync(id);
        claims = await ClaimsService.GetClaimsAsync();
    }
}
```

ClaimDetails.razor

The *ClaimDetails.razor* is a Blazor component that provides a user interface for viewing the details of a specific claim. It interacts with the ***ClaimsService*** to fetch and display claim details.

```
@page "/claim/{claimId}"
@using BenefitsManager.Frontend.WebPortal.Ui.Models
@using BenefitsManager.Frontend.WebPortal.Ui.Services
@using System.ComponentModel.DataAnnotations
@inject ClaimsService ClaimsService

<h3>Claims List</h3>

@if (claim == null)
{
    <p>Loading...</p>
}
else
{
    <div class="card">
        <div class="card-body">
            <h5 class="card-title">Claim from @claim.Merchant</h5>
            <p class="card-text">
                Claim ID: @claim.ClaimId<br />
                Claimed Amount: $@claim.ClaimedAmount<br />
```

CHAPTER 3 CREATING AND DEPLOYING FRONTEND – BLAZOR WEB APPLICATION

```
                Approved Amount: @(claim.ApprovedAmount.
                HasValue ? $"${claim.ApprovedAmount}" :
                "Pending")<br />
                Purchase Date:
                @(DateTimeOffset.FromUnixTimeMilliseconds
                (claim.PurchaseDate).DateTime.ToShortDate
                String())<br />
                Category: @claim.Category.CategoryName (@claim.
                Category.ParentCategoryName)<br />
                Description: @claim.Description<br />
                <a href="@claim.ReceiptPath" target="_
                blank">Download receipt</a>
            </p>
        </div>
    </div>
}

@code {
    [Parameter]
    [Required]
    public string claimId { get; set; }
    private ClaimModel claim;

    protected override async Task OnInitializedAsync()
    {
        Console.WriteLine($"Navigated to Claim: {claimId}");
        claim = await ClaimsService.GetClaimByIdAsync(new
        Guid(claimId));
    }
}
```

3.5.5 Program Configuration

The Program.cs file is the entry point of the BenefitsManager.Frontend. WebPortal.Ui project that sets up the web application, configures services, and defines HTTP request pipeline.

Register the *ClaimService* as a scoped service, which makes it available during dependency injection throughout the application. Also, configure logging to output debug level messages to the console during development.

```
using BenefitsManager.Frontend.WebPortal.Ui.Services;
using BenefitsManager.Frontend.WebPortal.Ui.Components;
using BenefitsManager.Frontend.WebPortal.Ui.Models;

var builder = WebApplication.CreateBuilder(args);

// Add services to the container.
builder.Services.AddRazorComponents()
    .AddInteractiveServerComponents();

var backendApiBaseUrlExternalHttp = builder.Configuration.GetValue<string>("BackendApiConfig:BaseUrlExternalHttp");

builder.Services.AddScoped(sp => new HttpClient { BaseAddress = new Uri(backendApiBaseUrlExternalHttp) });
builder.Services.AddScoped<ClaimsService>();

builder.Logging.SetMinimumLevel(LogLevel.Debug);
builder.Logging.AddConsole();

var app = builder.Build();

// Configure the HTTP request pipeline.
if (!app.Environment.IsDevelopment())
{
```

CHAPTER 3   CREATING AND DEPLOYING FRONTEND – BLAZOR WEB APPLICATION

```
    app.UseExceptionHandler("/Error", createScopeForErrors: 
        true);
    // The default HSTS value is 30 days. You may want to 
        change this for production scenarios, see https://aka.
        ms/aspnetcore-hsts.
    app.UseHsts();
}

app.UseHttpsRedirection();

app.UseStaticFiles();
app.UseAntiforgery();

app.MapRazorComponents<App>()
    .AddInteractiveServerRenderMode();

app.Run();
```

Add BaseUrlExternalHttp inside the appsettings.json file, which is used inside the Program.cs file.

Note   The above URL "http://localhost:5103/" is the endpoint for the backend API created in Chapter 2. Once the frontend web app is deployed to ACA, we will update this variable with production-ready backend service URL running as Azure container app.

```
{
  "Logging": {
    "LogLevel": {
      "Default": "Information",
      "Microsoft.AspNetCore": "Warning"
    }
  },
```

79

CHAPTER 3   CREATING AND DEPLOYING FRONTEND – BLAZOR WEB APPLICATION

```
  "AllowedHosts": "*",
  "BackendApiConfig":
  {
    "BaseUrlExternalHttp": "http://localhost:5103/"
  }
}
```

> **POINT TO NOTE**
>
> In this chapter, we will run multiple projects from Visual Studio and use the local backend service during development; however, we will replace it with the live production backend service URL running on Azure Container Apps once the frontend is also deployed to ACA.

3.6 Docker Configuration

To deploy the BenefitsClaimManager.Frontend application to Azure Container Apps, we need to containerize this application and push the container image to Azure Container Registry.

Open the VS Code Command Palette (Ctrl+Shift+P) and select Docker: Add Docker Files to Workspace….

- Use `.NET:ASP.NET Core` when prompted for the application platform.
- Choose the newly created project, if prompted.
- Choose `Linux` when prompted to choose the operating system.
- Set the application port to 5000. This is arbitrary but memorable for this workshop.

CHAPTER 3   CREATING AND DEPLOYING FRONTEND – BLAZOR WEB APPLICATION

- You will be asked if you want to add Docker Compose files. Select No.

- Dockerfile and .dockerignore files are added to the workspace.

Open Dockerfile and replace

```
FROM --platform=$BUILDPLATFORM mcr.microsoft.com/dotnet/sdk:9.0 AS build
```

with

```
FROM mcr.microsoft.com/dotnet/sdk:9.0 AS build
```

> **POINT TO NOTE**
>
> Azure Container Registry does not set $BUILDPLATFORM presently when building containers. This consequently causes the build to fail. See https://github.com/microsoft/vscode-docker/issues/4149 for details. Therefore, we removed it from the file as a workaround mentioned by the product team.

After modification, **Dockerfile** will look as shown below:

```
FROM mcr.microsoft.com/dotnet/aspnet:9.0 AS base
WORKDIR /app
EXPOSE 5000

ENV ASPNETCORE_URLS=http://+:5000

USER app
FROM mcr.microsoft.com/dotnet/sdk:9.0 AS build
ARG configuration=Release
WORKDIR /src
```

```
COPY ["BenefitsManager.Frontend.WebPortal.Ui/BenefitsManager.
Frontend.WebPortal.Ui.csproj", "BenefitsManager.Frontend.
WebPortal.Ui/"]
RUN dotnet restore "BenefitsManager.Frontend.WebPortal.Ui/
BenefitsManager.Frontend.WebPortal.Ui.csproj"
COPY . .
WORKDIR "/src/BenefitsManager.Frontend.WebPortal.Ui"
RUN dotnet build "BenefitsManager.Frontend.WebPortal.Ui.csproj"
-c $configuration -o /app/build

FROM build AS publish
ARG configuration=Release
RUN dotnet publish "BenefitsManager.Frontend.
WebPortal.Ui.csproj" -c $configuration -o /app/publish
/p:UseAppHost=false

FROM base AS final
WORKDIR /app
COPY --from=publish /app/publish .
ENTRYPOINT ["dotnet", "BenefitsManager.Frontend.WebPortal.
Ui.dll"]
```

3.7 Creating Azure Infrastructure

Now that we understand the code base, we can deploy the frontend web application to Azure Container Apps. If you have completed reading Chapter 2, most of the Azure infrastructure-related services are created, and we will reuse the same resource group.

3.7.1 Build and Publish the Docker Image

Build the *BenefitsManager.Frontend.WebPortal.Ui* project on Azure Container Registry (ACR) and push the Docker image to ACR. Use the below command to initiate the image build and push process using ACR. The "." at the end of the command represents the Docker build context; in our case, we need to be in the parent directory that hosts the .csproj.

```
$FE_WEB_UI_NAME = "ca-benefitsmanager-fe-ui"

az acr build `
--registry $AZURE_CONTAINER_REGISTRY_NAME `
--image "benefitsmanager/$FE_WEB_UI_NAME" `
--file 'BenefitsManager.Frontend.WebPortal.Ui/Dockerfile' .
```

Once this step is completed, you can verify the results by going to the Azure portal and checking that a new repository named **"benefitsmanager/ca-benefitsmanager-fe-ui"** has been created and that there is a new Docker image with a latest tag as shown in Figure 3-2.

CHAPTER 3   CREATING AND DEPLOYING FRONTEND – BLAZOR WEB APPLICATION

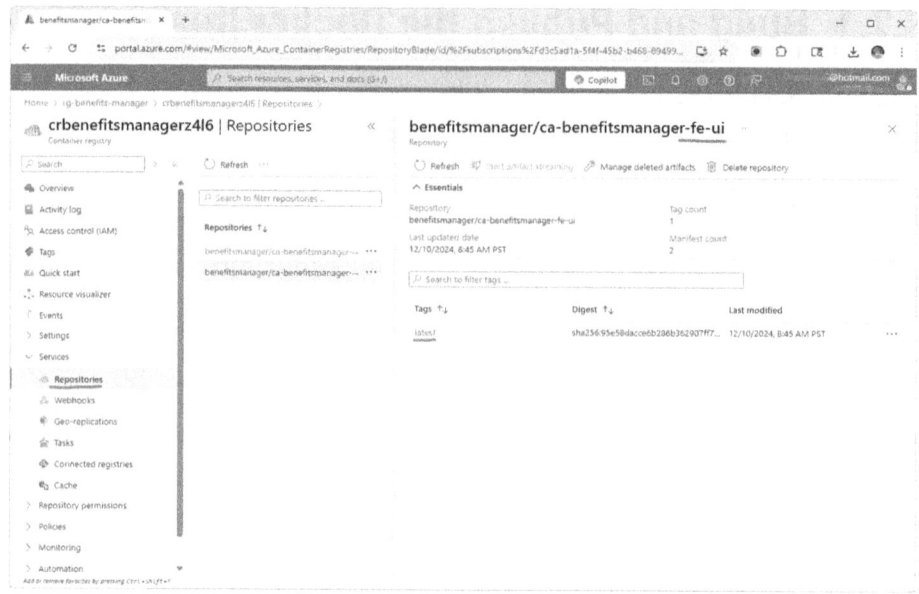

Figure 3-2. *ACR repository containing the latest Docker image*

3.7.2 Deploying to Azure Container Apps

The last step here is to create and deploy the web frontend application to ACA by running the command below:

```
$BACKEND_API_EXTERNAL_BASE_URL= "https://ca-benefitsmanager-bff-api.ashymushroom-0ed776ff.eastus.azurecontainerapps.io/"

$fqdn=(az containerapp create `
--name $FE_WEB_UI_NAME `
--resource-group $RESOURCE_GROUP `
--environment $ENVIRONMENT `
--image "$AZURE_CONTAINER_REGISTRY_NAME.azurecr.io/benefitsmanager/$FE_WEB_UI_NAME" `
```

```
--target-port $TARGET_PORT `
--ingress 'external' `
--min-replicas 1 `
--max-replicas 1 `
--cpu 0.25 `
--memory 0.5Gi `
--query properties.configuration.ingress.fqdn `
--output tsv)

$$FE_WEB_UI_NAME_BASE_URL="https://$fqdn"
```

3.7.3 Update the Backend Web API Container App Ingress Property

So far, the Frontend App is sending HTTP requests to the publicly exposed Web API. This means that any REST client can invoke the Web API. We need to change the Web API ingress settings and make it accessible only by applications deployed within our Azure Container Environment. Any application outside the Azure Container Environment should not be able to access the Web API.

To change the settings of the backend API, execute the following command:

```
$fqdn=(az containerapp ingress enable `
--name $BACKEND_API_NAME `
--resource-group $RESOURCE_GROUP `
--target-port $TARGET_PORT `
--type "internal" `
--query fqdn `
--output tsv)
```

CHAPTER 3   CREATING AND DEPLOYING FRONTEND – BLAZOR WEB APPLICATION

```
$BACKEND_API_INTERNAL_BASE_URL="https://$fqdn"

echo "The internal backend API URL:"
echo $BACKEND_API_INTERNAL_BASE_URL
```

The last thing we need to do here is to update the Frontend WebApp environment variable named **BackendApiConfig_BaseUrlExternalHttp** with the new value of the internal backend Web API–based URL; to do so, we need to update the web app container app, and it will create a new revision implicitly. The following command will update the container app with the changes:

```
az containerapp update `
--name "$FE_WEB_UI_NAME" `
--resource-group $RESOURCE_GROUP `
--set-env-vars "BackendApiConfig__BaseUrlExternalHttp=$BACKEND_API_INTERNAL_BASE_URL/"
```

On the Azure portal, you can verify this by navigating to the deployed frontend ACA. In the app's left menu, select **Revisions and replicas**, and select create new revision. Edit the current container image, and in the Environment variables section, you can see the updated environment variables as shown in Figure 3-3.

CHAPTER 3   CREATING AND DEPLOYING FRONTEND – BLAZOR WEB APPLICATION

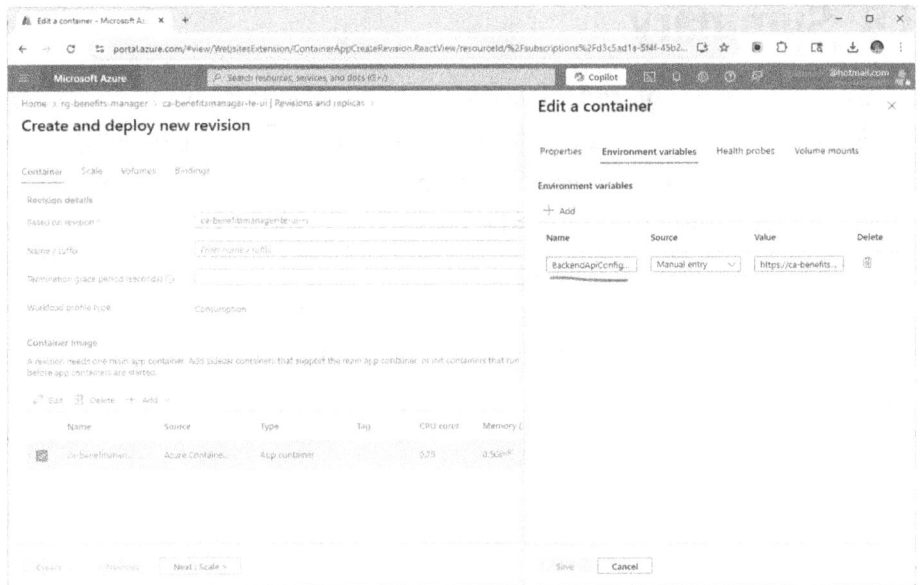

Figure 3-3. *Updated environment variables inside the container image*

Browse the frontend web application again, and you should be able to see the same results and access the backend API endpoints from the web app as shown in Figure 3-4. You can obtain the frontend URL from the above PowerShell code or by navigating to the Azure portal container app overview page.

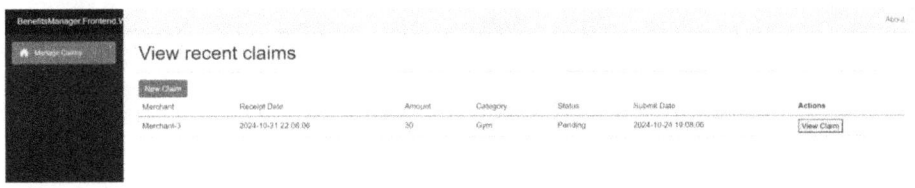

Figure 3-4. *Blazor frontend web app displaying recent claims*

87

3.8 Summary

In this chapter, we explored the creation and deployment of a Blazor web application to Azure Container Apps (ACA). We covered the development of Web - Frontend, containerizing the application, the deployment process to Azure, and the steps taken to secure the ACA API Backend from external access.

Additionally, we set the stage for further enhancement by introducing Dapr, focusing on service discovery and invocation in the upcoming chapters.

CHAPTER 4

Integrating Dapr with Azure Container Apps

In this chapter, you will be introduced to the **Distributed Application Runtime (Dapr)**, specifically on integrating with Azure Container Apps. Dapr is an open source, **portable**, **event-driven runtime** that makes it easy to build resilient, stateless, and stateful microservices. The learning objectives for this chapter include the following:

- Introduction to Dapr.
- Benefits of using Dapr integration with ACA.
- How to configure Dapr on a local dev machine.
- Best practices during Dapr integration.
- Decouple BenefitsManager.Frontend.WebPortal.Ui from BenefitsManager.Backend.Bff.Api locally via Dapr.
- Leverage Dapr State Management in BenefitsManager application.
- Provision Azure Cosmos DB as a state store.

CHAPTER 4   INTEGRATING DAPR WITH AZURE CONTAINER APPS

4.1 Introduction to Dapr

If you are a distributed systems developer working to create resilient, scalable distributed applications as microservices, you often face the same set of challenges over and over. Some of the challenges are as follows:

- How to recover the state after failures?
- How to manage secrets?
- How to discover other microservices and how to securely call them?

If our perspective resonates with you, you might ask, "Is there a solution?" The answer is yes. With Dapr, developers can focus solely on building their application code, leaving the complexities of distributed systems behind.

Dapr, which stands for Distributed Application Runtime, is an open source project that was launched by Microsoft as an incubation project in early 2019. It gained a lot of interest and support from the community. Dapr was later accepted into the Cloud Native Computing Foundation (CNCF) incubator on November 9, 2021, at the **incubating** maturity level and then moved to the **graduated** maturity level on October 30, 2024.

According to the official Dapr website:

> *Dapr is a portable, event-driven runtime that makes it easy for developers to build resilient, microservice stateless and stateful applications that run on the cloud and edge and embraces the diversity of languages and developer frameworks.*
>
> —dapr.io

Dapr adapts to your current environment, allowing you to use it with any language and development framework and deploy it anywhere, as illustrated in Figure 4-1.

CHAPTER 4 INTEGRATING DAPR WITH AZURE CONTAINER APPS

Figure 4-1. *Dapr language + framework support (Courtesy from Dapr official docs)*

At the heart of Dapr are the *building blocks* that encapsulate industry best practices and simplify the challenges faced when building microservices. Through building blocks, Dapr provides consistent APIs and abstracts away the implementation details to keep your code simple and portable.

In this book, we will integrate Dapr with Azure Container Apps and take advantage of some of these building blocks:

- **Service-to-Service Invocation**: Supports service-to-service communication with automatic retries, observability, and more

- **State Management**: Provides a consistent and reliable state store for managing your application state

- **Publish and Subscribe**: Enables publish/subscribe messaging between services

- **Bindings**: Connect to external systems like databases, message queues, and other cloud services

- **Workflows**: Automate and orchestrate tasks within your application

- **Jobs**: Scheduled tasks to run at specified intervals or at specified time

Let us explore endpoints for all the building blocks mentioned above in a table format as shown in Table 4-1.

Table 4-1. List of endpoints for various Dapr building blocks

Building Block	Endpoint	Description
Service-to-service invocation	/v1.0/invoke	Isss
State management	/v1.0/state	It enables storing state within a pluggable state store for persistence.
Publish and subscribe	/v1.0/publish /v1.0/subscribe	Pub/Sub is a loosely coupled messaging pattern where senders publish messages to a topic to which subscribers subscribe.
Bindings	/v1.0/bindings	It provides bidirectional connection to an external cloud/on-premises service or system.
Workflows	/v1.0-beta1/workflow	The workflow API enables you to define long-running, persistent processes or data flows that span multiple microservices using Dapr workflows or workflow components.
Jobs	/v1.0-alpha1/jobs	The Jobs API enables you to schedule and orchestrate jobs. **Example:** Schedule batch processing job to run every business day.

You can integrate Dapr into existing applications by starting with a single building block and gradually adding more as needed.

Let's say you are building an app that requires you to store state; using the simple state management API, you can quickly create long-running resilient stateful services. Dapr handles the heavy lifting, keeping your code simple and agnostic to any specific store implementation. This allows you to easily swap out the underlying components without changing the code.

How does it work? In a nutshell, Dapr runs along with your application as a sidecar whether on your local dev machine or on edge or on cloud. When hosting your application on Kubernetes, Dapr runs as another container inside your Pod. When your application scales, Dapr scales with it.

4.2 Benefits of Integrating Dapr in Azure Container Apps

The *Benefits Manager* microservice application is composed of multiple microservices. Function calls are spread across the network. To support the distributed nature of microservices, we need to account for failures, retries, and timeouts. While Azure Container Apps feature the building blocks for running microservices, using the Distributed Application Runtime (Dapr) provides an even richer microservices programming model.

Dapr includes features like service discovery, Pub/Sub, service-to-service invocation with mutual TLS, retries, state store management, and more. Because the calls will flow through container sidecars, Dapr can inject some useful cross-cutting behaviors that are meaningfully abstracted from our application containers.

Although we won't tap into all these benefits of Dapr, it's worth noting that you will probably rely on these features in this book:

- Automatically retry calls upon failure.

- Make calls between services secured with mutual authentication (mTLS), including automatic certificate rollover.

- Control what operations clients can perform using access control policies.

- Capture traces and metrics for all calls between services to provide insights and diagnostics.

> **POINT TO NOTE**
>
> This chapter provides an overview of Dapr; however, if you want to deep dive and learn more about Dapr, I highly recommend the book *Introducing Distributed Application Runtime (Dapr)* from Apress: `https://link.springer.com/book/10.1007/978-1-4842-6998-5`.

4.3 Configure Dapr on a Local Development Machine

To run applications using Dapr, we need to install and initialize Dapr CLI locally. The official documentation is quite clear (refer to `https://docs.dapr.io/getting-started/install-dapr-cli/`), and you can follow the steps needed based on your machine operating system.

Install Dapr CLI on Windows Machine

Install the latest Windows Dapr CLI to $Env:SystemDrive\dapr and add this directory to the user PATH environment variable:

powershell -Command "iwr -useb https://raw.githubusercontent.com/dapr/cli/master/install/install.ps1 | iex"

Install Using winget

Install the latest Windows Dapr CLI to $Env:SystemDrive\dapr and add this directory to the user PATH environment variable by running the below command:

winget install Dapr.CLI

Expected output:

```
C:\Windows\System32>winget install Dapr.CLI
Found Dapr CLI [Dapr.CLI] Version 1.14.1
This application is licensed to you by its owner.
Microsoft is not responsible for, nor does it grant any licenses to, third-party packages.
Downloading https://github.com/dapr/cli/releases/download/v1.14.1/dapr.msi
                                   36.0 MB / 36.0 MB
Successfully verified installer hash
Starting package install...
Successfully installed
```

Verify that the CLI is installed by restarting your terminal/command prompt, and running the following command will show output as shown in Figure 4-2.

dapr -h

Expected output:

```
C:\>dapr -h


      __
  ___/ /___ _____  _____
 / __  / __ `/ __ \/ ___/
/ /_/ / /_/ / /_/ / /
\__,_/\__,_/ .___/_/
          /_/

===============================
Distributed Application Runtime

Usage:
  dapr [flags]
  dapr [command]

Available Commands:
  annotate        Add dapr annotations to a Kubernetes configuration. Supported platforms: Kubernetes
  build-info      Print build info of Dapr CLI and runtime
  completion      Generates shell completion scripts
  components      List all Dapr components. Supported platforms: Kubernetes
  configurations  List all Dapr configurations. Supported platforms: Kubernetes
  dashboard       Start Dapr dashboard. Supported platforms: Kubernetes and self-hosted
  help            Help about any command
  init            Install Dapr on supported hosting platforms. Supported platforms: Kubernetes and self-hosted
  invoke          Invoke a method on a given Dapr application. Supported platforms: Self-hosted
  list            List all Dapr instances. Supported platforms: Kubernetes
  logs            Get Dapr sidecar logs for an application. Supported platforms: Kubernetes
  mtls            Check if mTLS is enabled. Supported platforms: Kubernetes
  publish         Publish a pub-sub event. Supported platforms: Self-hosted
  run             Run Dapr and (optionally) your application side by side. Supported platforms: Self-hosted
  status          Show the health status of Dapr services. Supported platforms: Kubernetes
  stop            Stop Dapr instances and their associated apps. Supported platforms: Self-hosted
  uninstall       Uninstall Dapr runtime. Supported platforms: Kubernetes and self-hosted
  upgrade         Upgrades or downgrades a Dapr control plane installation in a cluster. Supported platforms: Kubernetes     version    Print the Da
pr runtime and CLI version

Flags:
  -h, --help                  help for dapr
      --log-as-json           Log output in JSON format
      --runtime-path string   The path to the dapr runtime installation directory
  -v, --version               version for dapr

Use "dapr [command] --help" for more information about a command.
```

Figure 4-2. *Dapr help command output*

Now that you've verified the installation of Dapr CLI, use the CLI to initialize Dapr runtime binaries on your local machine by running the below command:

dapr init

Expected output:

```
C:\Windows\System32>dapr init
Making the jump to hyperspace...
Container images will be pulled from Docker Hub
Installing runtime version 1.14.4
Downloading binaries and setting up components...
Downloaded binaries and completed components set up.
daprd binary has been installed to C:\Users\nagavo\.dapr\bin.
dapr_placement container is running.
dapr_redis container is running.
dapr_zipkin container is running.
dapr_scheduler container is running.
Use `docker ps` to check running containers.
Success! Dapr is up and running. To get started, go here: https://docs.dapr.io/getting-started
```

Verify the Dapr version by running the below command:

dapr -version

which displays the installed CLI and runtime versions:

```
C:\Windows\System32>dapr --version
CLI version: 1.14.1
Runtime version: 1.14.4
```

4.4 Configure Backend API Locally via Dapr

We are now ready to run the applications locally using the Dapr sidecar in a self-hosted mode. The Dapr VS Code extension (refer to https://marketplace.visualstudio.com/items?itemName=ms-azuretools.vscode-dapr) will allow you to run, debug, and interact with Dapr-enabled applications.

Create variables to capture both frontend and backend localhost ports from launchSettings.json file as shown in Figure 4-3.

```
$API_APP_PORT=<web api https port in Properties->launchSettings.json (e.g. 7219)>
$UI_APP_PORT=<web ui https port in Properties->launchSettings.json (e.g. 7000)>
```

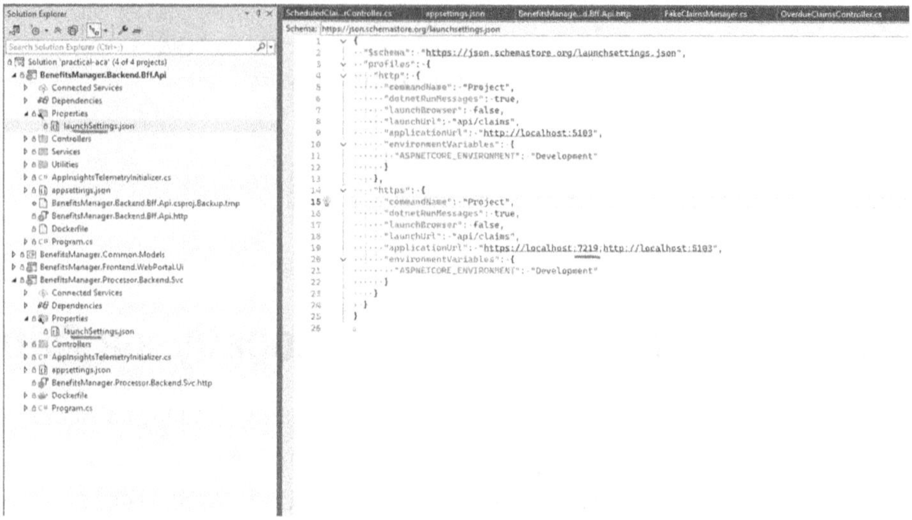

CHAPTER 4   INTEGRATING DAPR WITH AZURE CONTAINER APPS

Figure 4-3. launchSettings.json file of backend API

Run the below "**dapr run**" command to run BenefitsManager.Backend. Bff.Api backend service locally:

```
Cd ~/BenefitsManager.Backend.BFF.API
dapr run `
--app-id BenefitsManager-Backend-Bff-Api `
--app-port $API_APP_PORT `
--dapr-http-port 3500 `
--app-ssl `
-- dotnet run --launch-profile https
```

If all is working as expected, you should receive an output similar to the one below where your app logs and Dapr logs will appear on the same PowerShell terminal as shown in Figure 4-4.

CHAPTER 4 INTEGRATING DAPR WITH AZURE CONTAINER APPS

Figure 4-4. Successful output message from the Dapr run command

Now to test invoking the web API using the Dapr sidecar, you can issue a **GET** request to the following URL:

http://localhost:3500/v1.0/invoke/BenefitsManager-Backend-Bff-Api/method/api/claims/?userId=user3@mail.com

Successful web request returns **200 Ok status** as shown in Figure 4-5.

CHAPTER 4   INTEGRATING DAPR WITH AZURE CONTAINER APPS

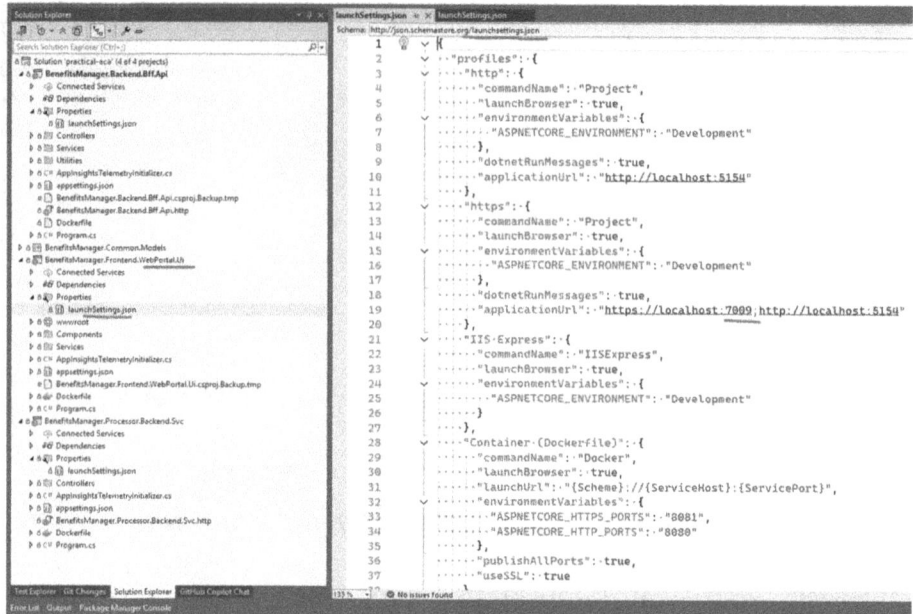

Figure 4-5. *200 Ok status returned from the GET web request*

4.5 Configure ACA Web - Frontend Locally via Dapr

We will be using the Dapr SDK (refer to https://github.com/dapr/dotnet-sdk) in the frontend web app to invoke backend API services. The Dapr .NET SDK provides .NET developers with an intuitive and language-specific way to interact with Dapr. The SDK offers developers three ways of making remote service invocation calls:

- Invoke HTTP services using HttpClient
- Invoke HTTP services using DaprClient
- Invoke gRPC services using DaprClient

CHAPTER 4   INTEGRATING DAPR WITH AZURE CONTAINER APPS

We will be using the second approach in this book (HTTP services using DaprClient).

Install Dapr SDK for .NET Core in the frontend web app, so we can use the service discovery and service invocation offered by the Dapr sidecar. To accomplish this, add the following NuGet package to the project:

```
<ItemGroup>
  <PackageReference Include="Dapr.AspNetCore"
  Version="1.14.0" />
</ItemGroup>
```

Open the file Program.cs of the Frontend "BenefitsManager.Frontend. WebPortal.Ui" and register the DaprClient as shown below:

```
// Add Dapr client
builder.Services.AddDaprClient();
```

Now, we will inject the DaprClient into the ClaimService.cs class to use the method **InvokeMethodAsync** to make a call to the Dapr sidecar endpoint running on port 3500.

```
using BenefitsManager.Frontend.WebPortal.Ui.Models;
using Dapr.Client;

namespace BenefitsManager.Frontend.WebPortal.Ui.Services
{
    public class ClaimServices
    {
        private readonly HttpClient _httpClient;
        private readonly DaprClient _daprClient;

        public ClaimServices(HttpClient httpClient, DaprClient daprClient)
```

```csharp
{
    _httpClient = httpClient;
    _daprClient = daprClient;
}

public async Task<List<Claim>> GetClaimsAsync()
{
    return await _daprClient.InvokeMethodAsync<List
    <Claim>>(
        HttpMethod.Get,
        "BenefitsManager-Backend-Bff-Api",
        "api/claims/?userId=user3@mail.com"
    );
}

public async Task<Claim> GetClaimByIdAsync(int id)
{
    return await _daprClient.InvokeMethodAsync<Claim>(
        HttpMethod.Get,
        "BenefitsManager-Backend-Bff-Api",
        $"api/claims/{id}"
    );
}

public async Task CreateClaimAsync(Claim claim)
{
    await _daprClient.InvokeMethodAsync(
        HttpMethod.Post,
        "BenefitsManager-Backend-Bff-Api",
        "api/claims",
        claim
    );
}
```

```csharp
public async Task UpdateClaimAsync(Claim claim)
{
    await _daprClient.InvokeMethodAsync(
        HttpMethod.Put,
        "BenefitsManager-Backend-Bff-Api",
        $"api/claims/{claim}",
        claim
    );
}
public async Task DeleteClaimAsync(Guid id)
{
    await _daprClient.InvokeMethodAsync(
        HttpMethod.Delete,
        "BenefitsManager-Backend-Bff-Api",
        $"api/claims/{id}"
    );
}
    }
}
```

Notice how we are not using the HttpClient anymore and how we were able to use frontend Dapr sidecar to invoke backend API sidecar using the method InvokeMethodAsync, which accepts the Dapr **remote App ID** for the backend API BenefitsManager-Backend-Bff-Api, and it will be able to discover the URL and invoke the method based on the specified input params.

In addition to this, notice how in POST and PUT operations the fourth argument is a Claim Model; this will be serialized internally (using System.Text.JsonSerializer) and sent as the request payload. The .NET SDK takes care of the call to the sidecar. It also deserializes the response in case of the GET operations to a List<Claim> object.

Looking at the first option of invoking the remote service, "Invoke HTTP services using HttpClient", you can see that we can create an HttpClient by invoking `DaprClient.CreateInvokeHttpClient`, specify the remote service app id and custom port if needed, and then use the HTTP methods such as `GetFromJsonAsync`; this is a good approach as well as it gives you full support of advanced scenarios, such as custom headers, and full control over request and response messages.

In both options, the final request will be rewritten by the Dapr .NET SDK before it gets executed. In our case and for the GET operation, it will be written to this request: `http://127.0.0.1:3500/v1.0/invoke/BenefitsManager-Backend-Bff-Api/method/api/claims/?userId=user3@mail.com`.

4.6 Run ACA Web - Frontend and ACA API Backend Locally Using Dapr

We are now ready to verify the changes on the frontend web app and test it locally. We need to run the frontend web app along with the Backend Web API to ensure the Dapr sidecar containers are working as expected.

Open another terminal so that we can run the two commands shown below (ensure that you are on the right project directory when running each command).

Obtain the local frontend UI URL from the launchSettings.json file as shown in Figure 4-6.

```
$API_APP_PORT=<web api https port in Properties->launchSettings.json (e.g. 7112)>
$UI_APP_PORT=<web ui https port in Properties->launchSettings.json (e.g. 7000)>
```

CHAPTER 4   INTEGRATING DAPR WITH AZURE CONTAINER APPS

Figure 4-6. *launchSettings.json file of frontend UI*

In each of the two terminals previously opened, run the frontend UI and backend API, respectively.

```
dapr run `
--app-id BenefitsManager-Backend-Bff-Api `
--app-port $API_APP_PORT `
--dapr-http-port 3500 `
--app-ssl `
-- dotnet run --launch-profile https
dapr run `
--app-id BenefitsManager-Frontend-WebPortal-Ui `
--app-port $UI_APP_PORT `
--dapr-http-port 3501 `
--app-ssl `
-- dotnet run --launch-profile https
```

Notice how we assigned the Dapr App Id "BenefitsManager-Frontend-WebPortal-Ui" to the frontend web application.

105

CHAPTER 4   INTEGRATING DAPR WITH AZURE CONTAINER APPS

> **POINT TO NOTE**
>
> If you need to run both microservices together, you need to keep calling `dapr run` manually each time in the terminal. And when you have multiple microservices talking to each other, you need to run at the same time to debug the solution. This can be a convoluted process. In the next chapter, we will discuss how to configure VS Code for running and debugging Dapr applications.

4.7 Test ACA Web - Frontend and ACA API Backend Locally Using Dapr

Both applications are running using the Dapr sidecar. Note how ports 3500 and 3501 are used when starting the container apps. These ports instruct the container runtime to communicate with the Dapr sidecar, whereas the https ports from the appsettings files are the ports you use to launch the application locally. Open the local frontend UI URL (use $FRONTEND_UI_BASE_URL_LOCAL from Section 4.5); ignore the certificate warning locally. If the application is working as expected, you should see the Claims list associated with the email (user3@mail.com) you provided as shown in Figure 4-7.

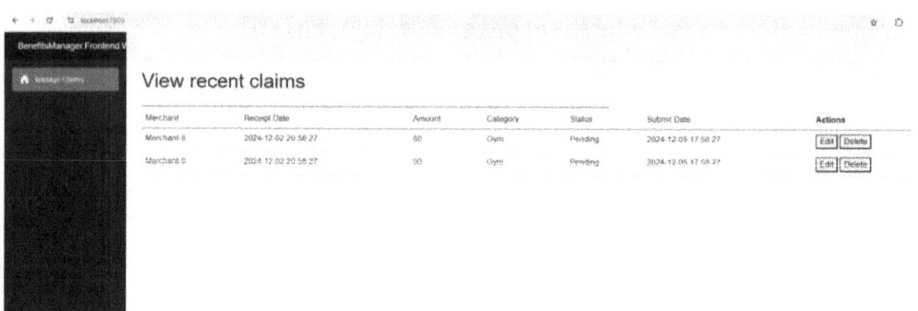

Figure 4-7. *Web frontend talking to the Dapr sidecar API endpoint*

> **Note** If you started the Dapr Instance directly in the PowerShell terminal, you could simply press Ctrl+C to interrupt and stop it.

4.8 Debug and Launch Dapr Applications in VS Code

Instead of using individual PowerShell windows to run Dapr, we can configure VS Code to run and debug multiple Dapr applications at the same time.

We need to update VS Code **tasks.json** and **launch.json** configuration files included in your workspace. Once completed, you should be able to use the Run and Debug button on the activity bar within VS Code to launch all services to be able to debug them locally.

First, we need to add a new launch configuration for the Backend Web API and frontend web app projects. To accomplish this, open file launch.json and add the two configurations shown below.

launch.json

```
{
            "name": "Launch (backend api) with Dapr",
            "type": "node",
            "request": "launch",
            "preLaunchTask": "backend-api-dapr-debug",
            "program": "${workspaceFolder}/BenefitsManager.Backend.Bff.Api/bin/Debug/net9.0/BenefitsManager.Backend.Bff.Api.dll",
            "args": [],
            "cwd": "${workspaceFolder}/BenefitsManager.Backend.Bff.Api",
```

```
            "serverReadyAction": {
                "action": "openExternally",
                "pattern": "\\bNow listening on:\\
                s+(https?://\\S+)"
            },
            "env": {
                "ASPNETCORE_ENVIRONMENT": "Development"
            },
            "postDebugTask": "daprd-down-backend-api"
        },
        {
            "name": "Launch (web app) with Dapr",
            "type": "node",
            "request": "launch",
            "preLaunchTask": "webapp-ui-dapr-debug",
            "program": "${workspaceFolder}/BenefitsManager.
            Frontend.WebPortal.Ui/bin/Debug/net9.0/
            BenefitsManager.Frontend.WebPortal.Ui.dll",
            "args": [],
            "cwd": "${workspaceFolder}/BenefitsManager.
            Frontend.WebPortal.Ui",
            "serverReadyAction": {
                "action": "openExternally",
                "pattern": "\\bNow listening on:\\
                s+(https?://\\S+)"
            },
            "env": {
                "ASPNETCORE_ENVIRONMENT": "Development"
            },
            "postDebugTask": "webapp-ui-daprd-down"
        },
```

tasks.json

```json
{
        "appId": "BenefitsManager-Backend-Bff-Api",
        "appPort": 7219,
        "httpPort": 3500,
        "grpcPort": 50001,
        "appSsl": true,
        "label": "backend-api-dapr-debug",
        "type": "dapr",
        "dependsOn": "build-backend-api",
        // Uncomment this line after adding Azure Cosmos DB
           to the state store yaml file
        "componentsPath": "./components"
    },
    {
        "appId": "BenefitsManager-Backend-Bff-Api",
        "label": "daprd-down-backend-api",
        "type": "daprd-down"
    },
    {
        "appId": "BenefitsManager-Frontend-WebPortal-Ui",
        "appPort": 7009,
        "httpPort": 3501,
        "grpcPort": 50002,
        "appSsl": true,
        "label": "webapp-ui-dapr-debug",
        "type": "dapr",
        "dependsOn": "build-webapp-ui"
    },
    {
        "appId": "BenefitsManager-Frontend-WebPortal-Ui",
```

```
            "label": "webapp-ui-daprd-down",
            "type": "daprd-down"
        },
```

Lastly, we need to add a compound launch property, so we launch and debug both applications together.

Open the launch.json file and append the following array to the configuration array:

```
. "compounds": [
    {
        "name": "RunAll with Dapr",
        "configurations": [
            "Launch (backend api) with Dapr",
            "Launch (web app) with Dapr"
        ],
        "stopAll": true
    }
]
```

4.9 Overview of Dapr State Management API

By using the **Dapr State Management building block** (refer to https://docs.dapr.io/developing-applications/building-blocks/state-management/state-management-overview/), we will explore how we can store the data in Azure Cosmos DB without installing any Cosmos DB SDK or write specific code to integrate our backend API with Azure Cosmos DB. Moreover, we will use Redis to store claims when we are running the application locally. By the end of this chapter, you will learn how easy it is to switch between different stores without any code changes, thanks to the Dapr pluggable state stores features. By adding a new Dapr component

file, the underlying store will be changed (refer to https://docs.dapr.
io/reference/components-reference/supported-state-stores/ to see
the list of state stores supported by Dapr). Figure 4-8 shows how Dapr is
integrated between Web API Backend and Cosmos DB.

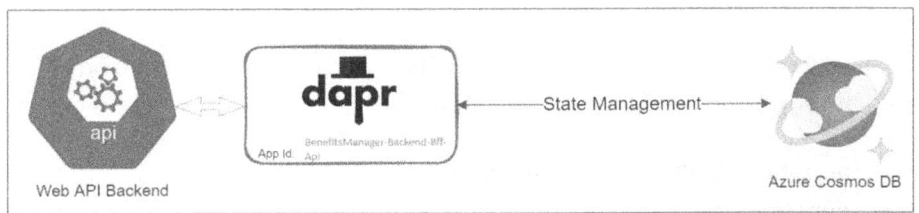

Figure 4-8. *Dapr state management for Web API Backend*

Dapr's state management API allows you to save, read, and query
key/value pairs in the supported state stores. To try this out, and without
making any code changes or installing any NuGet packages, we can
directly invoke the state management API and store the data on Redis
locally. When you initialized Dapr in your local development environment,
it installed the Redis container instance locally. So we can use Redis locally
to store and retrieve state. If you navigate to the path **%USERPROFILE%\.
dapr\components** (assuming you are using Windows), you will find a file
named statestore.yaml. Inside this file, you will see the properties needed
to access the local Redis instance as shown below:

```
apiVersion: dapr.io/v1alpha1
kind: Component
metadata:
  name: statestore
spec:
  type: state.redis
  version: v1
  metadata:
  - name: redisHost
```

CHAPTER 4   INTEGRATING DAPR WITH AZURE CONTAINER APPS

```
    value: localhost:6379
  - name: redisPassword
    value: ""
  - name: actorStateStore
    value: "true"
```

To try out the state management APIs, run the backend API from VS Code by running the following command:

```
Cd ~/BenefitsManager.Backend.BFF.API
dapr run `
--app-id BenefitsManager-Backend-Bff-Api `
--app-port $API_APP_PORT `
--dapr-http-port 3500 `
--app-ssl `
-- dotnet run --launch-profile https
```

Now from any rest client, invoke the below POST request to the endpoint http://localhost:3500/v1.0/state/statestore:

```
POST http://localhost:3500/v1.0/state/statestore
Host: localhost:3500
Content-Type: application/json
[
  {
    "key": "Claim1",
    "value": {
      "claimId": "59E029B1-1621-45A1-8263-A77AA7758FAE",
      "merchant": "Merchant-10",
      "claimedAmount": 80,
      "approvedAmount": null,
      "purchaseDate": 1733201907427,
      "category": {
        "categoryCode": "CAT004",
```

```
      "parentCategoryName": "Fitness Activities",
      "categoryName": "Gym"
    },
    "description": "Random description2",
    "statusLog": [
      {
        "status": 0,
        "comment": "",
        "setBy": {
          "id": "323a3afe-711f-4aa6-80d0-f848d24a5340",
          "email": "user3@mail.com",
          "name": "User-3"
        },
        "ts": 1733450307427
      }
    ],
    "currentStatus": 0,
    "receiptPath": "https://storage.blob.core.windows.net/
    claims/63105a50-e295-4619-8708-c790601c976d/receipt.pdf",
    "createdBy": {
      "id": "323a3afe-711f-4aa6-80d0-f848d24a5340",
      "email": "user3@mail.com",
      "name": "User-3"
    },
    "createdOn": 1733450307427,
    "modifiedOn": null
  }
},
{
  "key": "Claim2",
  "value": {
```

```
    "claimId": "572F81CE-BE0E-49CA-BAD4-E6B92E4411F2",
    "merchant": "Merchant-11",
    "claimedAmount": 90,
    "approvedAmount": null,
    "purchaseDate": 1733201907427,
    "category": {
      "categoryCode": "CAT005",
      "parentCategoryName": "Fitness Activities",
      "categoryName": "Gym"
    },
    "description": "Random description4",
    "statusLog": [
      {
        "status": 0,
        "comment": "",
        "setBy": {
          "id": "323a3afe-711f-4aa6-80d0-f848d24a5340",
          "email": "user3@mail.com",
          "name": "User-3"
        },
        "ts": 1733450307427
      }
    ],
    "currentStatus": 0,
    "receiptPath": "https://storage.blob.core.windows.net/
    claims/bf6e5ec8-852d-4103-a3ce-cbc089b8691b/receipt.pdf",
    "createdBy": {
      "id": "323a3afe-711f-4aa6-80d0-f848d24a5340",
      "email": "user3@mail.com",
      "name": "User-3"
    },
```

        "createdOn": 1733450307427,
        "modifiedOn": null
      }
    }
]

You should see HTTP 204 No Content response as shown in Figure 4-9. The value **"statestore"** in the endpoint should match the **name** value in the global component file **"statestore.yaml"**. We have sent a request to store two claims; you can put any JSON representation in the value property as shown below.

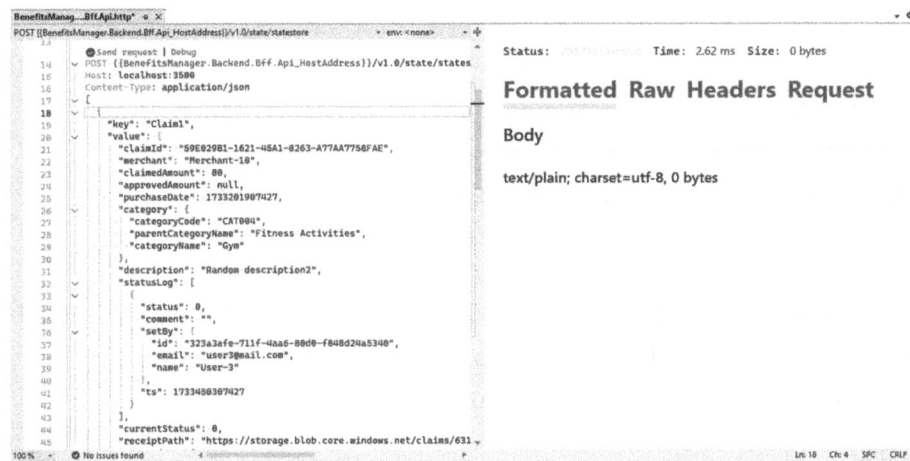

Figure 4-9. *Sending HTTP request to state store API endpoint, which returns 204 status*

Local Redis Cache

To see the results visually, you can install a VS Code extension to connect to Redis DB and see the results. There are several Redis extensions available for VS Code. We will use an extension named **"Redis Xplorer".**

Once you install the extension, it will add a tab under the explorer section of VS Code called "REDIS XPLORER". Next you will need to connect

Chapter 4 Integrating Dapr with Azure Container Apps

to the Redis server locally by adding a new "REDIS XPLORER" profile. Click on the + sign in the "REDIS XPLORER" section in VS Code. This will ask you to enter the nickname (e.g., dapr_redis) as well as the hostname and port. For the hostname and port, you can get this information by executing the following command in your PowerShell terminal:

docker ps

Look under the Ports column and use the server and port specified there. In Figure 4-10, the server is 0.0.0.0 and the port is 6379. Use the values that you see on your own terminal. Leave the password empty.

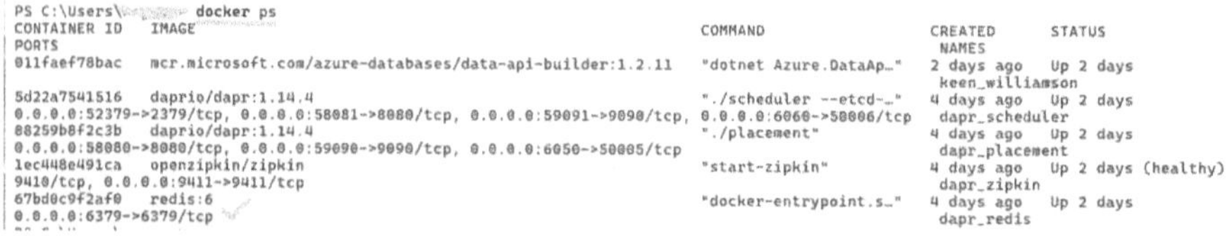

Figure 4-10. List of Docker containers up and running

After you connect to Redis locally, you should see two entries similar to the ones shown in Figure 4-11. Notice how each entry key is prefixed by the Dapr App Id followed by Key. In our case, it is **BenefitsManager-Backend-Bff-Api**.

Figure 4-11. *REDIS XPLORER, showing the list of claims submitted to local Redis cache*

To get the value of a key, you need to issue a GET request to the endpoint http://localhost:3500/v1.0/state/statestore/{YourKey}. This will return the value from the key store. For example, if you execute the GET http://localhost:3500/v1.0/state/statestore/Claim1, the results will be as shown in Figure 4-12.

CHAPTER 4   INTEGRATING DAPR WITH AZURE CONTAINER APPS

Figure 4-12. *HTTP GET request to retrieve the value of Claim2 key*

4.10 Use Dapr Client SDK for State Store Management

In the previous section, we demonstrated using Dapr State Store without code changes; we will now introduce a change on the backend API and create a new service named **ClaimsBenefitsManager.cs**, which will implement the interface **IClaimsManager.cs** to start storing claims data on the persist store. Locally, we will start testing with Redis; then we are going to change the state store to use Azure Cosmos DB.

4.10.1 Add Dapr Client SDK to the Backend API Project

Similar to what we have done in the frontend web app, we need to use Dapr Client SDK to manage the state store. Update the backend *.csproj file to add Dapr package reference.

```
<PackageReference Include="Dapr.AspNetCore" Version="1.14.0" />
```

4.10.2 Create a New Concrete Implementation to Manage Claims Persistence

In the previous chapters, we were storing Claims in memory using FakeClaimsManager.cs; now we need to store them in Redis and, later on, Azure Cosmos DB. The key thing to keep in mind here is that switching from Redis to Azure Cosmos DB won't require changing the code below, which is a huge advantage of using Dapr.

Add the file below to the **Services** folder. This file will implement the interface **IClaimsManager.cs**.

```
using BenefitsManager.Backend.Bff.Api.Common;
using BenefitsManager.Backend.Bff.Api.Models;
using Dapr.Client;

namespace BenefitsManager.Backend.Bff.Api.Services
{
    /// <summary>
    /// Manages the claims store which implements the
    IClaimsManager interface for storing claims in the Dapr
    State store.
    /// </summary>
    public class ClaimsStoreManager :IClaimsManager
    {
        private static string STORE_NAME = "statestore";
        private readonly DaprClient _daprClient;
        private readonly IConfiguration _config;
        private readonly ILogger<ClaimsStoreManager> _logger;
        private readonly List<ClaimCategoryModel> _
        claimCategoriesList = new List<ClaimCategoryModel>();
```

CHAPTER 4 INTEGRATING DAPR WITH AZURE CONTAINER APPS

```csharp
public ClaimsStoreManager(DaprClient daprClient, 
IConfiguration config, ILogger<ClaimsStore
Manager> logger)
{
    _daprClient = daprClient;
    _config = config;
    _logger = logger;

    GenerateRandomCategories();
}

private void GenerateRandomCategories()
{
    var categories = new List<ClaimCategoryModel>
    {
        new ClaimCategoryModel { CategoryCode = 
        "CAT001", ParentCategoryName = "Clothing 
        and shoes", CategoryName = "Athletic 
        Accessories" },
        new ClaimCategoryModel { CategoryCode = 
        "CAT002", ParentCategoryName = "Clothing and 
        shoes", CategoryName = "Athletic Apparel" },
        new ClaimCategoryModel { CategoryCode = 
        "CAT003", ParentCategoryName = "Fitness 
        Activities", CategoryName = "Gym" },
        new ClaimCategoryModel { CategoryCode = 
        "CAT004", ParentCategoryName = "Fitness 
        Activities", CategoryName = "Fitness 
        Classes" },
        new ClaimCategoryModel { CategoryCode = 
        "CAT005", ParentCategoryName = "Home Office", 
        CategoryName = "Desks and Chairs" }
    };
```

```csharp
    _claimCategoriesList.AddRange(categories);
}

public async Task<Guid> CreateNewClaimAsync(string 
merchant, decimal claimedAmount, long purchaseDate, 
string categoryCode, string description, string 
receiptPath, UserModel createdBy)
{
    var randomNo = Random.Shared.Next(1, 6);

    var claimId = Guid.NewGuid();
    var claim = new ClaimModel
    {
        ClaimId = claimId,
        Merchant = merchant,
        ClaimedAmount = claimedAmount,
        PurchaseDate = purchaseDate,
        Category = _claimCategoriesList.First(c =>
        c.CategoryCode == categoryCode),
        Description = description,
        StatusLog = new List<ClaimStatusModel>
        {
            new ClaimStatusModel
            {
                Status = ClaimStatus.Pending,
                Comment = "",
                SetBy = createdBy,
                Ts = DateTimeOffset.Now.
                ToUnixTimeMilliseconds()
            }
        },
```

```
            CurrentStatus = ClaimStatus.Pending,
            ReceiptPath = receiptPath,
            CreatedBy = createdBy,
            ApprovedAmount = null,
            CreatedOn = DateTimeOffset.Now.
            ToUnixTimeMilliseconds(),
            ModifiedOn = null
        };
        _logger.LogInformation("Save a new claim with id:
        '{0}' to state store", claim.ClaimId);
        await _daprClient.SaveStateAsync(STORE_NAME,
        claimId.ToString(), claim);
        return claimId;
    }

    public async Task<bool> DeleteClaimAsync(Guid claimId)
    {
        await _daprClient.DeleteStateAsync(STORE_NAME,
        claimId.ToString());
        return true;
    }

    public async Task<List<ClaimModel>>
    GetClaimsByCreatorAsync(string userId)
    {
        var state = await _daprClient.GetStateEntryAsync
        <List<ClaimModel>>(STORE_NAME, userId);
        return state.Value ?? new List<ClaimModel>();
    }

    public async Task<ClaimModel?> GetClaimByIdAsync
    (Guid claimId)
    {
```

```csharp
        var state = await _daprClient.GetStateEntryAsync
        <ClaimModel>(STORE_NAME, claimId.ToString());
        return state.Value;
    }

    public async Task<bool> UpdateClaimAsync(Guid
    claimId, string merchant, decimal claimedAmount, long
    purchaseDate, string categoryCode, string description,
    string receiptPath)
    {
        var state = await _daprClient.GetStateEntryAsync
        <ClaimModel>(STORE_NAME, claimId.ToString());
        if (state.Value == null)
        {
            return false;
        }
        state.Value.Merchant = merchant;
        state.Value.ClaimedAmount = claimedAmount;
        state.Value.PurchaseDate = purchaseDate;
        state.Value.Category = _claimCategoriesList.First
        (c => c.CategoryCode == categoryCode);
        state.Value.Description = description;
        state.Value.ReceiptPath = receiptPath;
        state.Value.ModifiedOn = DateTimeOffset.Now.
        ToUnixTimeMilliseconds();
        await state.SaveAsync();
        return true;
    }

    public async Task<bool> UpdateClaimStatusAsync(Guid
    claimId, decimal approvedAmount, ClaimStatus newStatus,
    string comment, UserModel setBy)
    {
```

CHAPTER 4 INTEGRATING DAPR WITH AZURE CONTAINER APPS

```
            var state = await _daprClient.GetStateEntryAsync
            <ClaimModel>(STORE_NAME, claimId.ToString());
            if (state.Value == null)
            {
                return false;
            }
            state.Value.CurrentStatus = newStatus;
            state.Value.ApprovedAmount = approvedAmount;
            state.Value.StatusLog.Add(new ClaimStatusModel
            {
                Status = newStatus,
                Comment = comment,
                SetBy = setBy,
                Ts = DateTimeOffset.Now.ToUnixTimeMilli
            seconds()
            });
            await state.SaveAsync();
            return true;
        }
    }
}
```

4.10.3 Register the ClaimsStoreManager New Service and DaprClient

We need to register the new service named ClaimsStoreManager and DaprClient when the backend API app starts up. Update the Program.cs file with the highlighted text as shown below:

```
//Add Dapr client
builder.Services.AddDaprClient();
```

```
// Add services to the container.
builder.Services.AddSingleton<IClaimsManager,
ClaimsStoreManager>();
//builder.Services.AddSingleton<IClaimsManager,
FakeClaimsManager>();
```

> **POINT TO NOTE**
>
> Do not forget to comment out the registration of the FakeClaimsManager Service as we don't want to store Claims in memory anymore.

Let's verify that the Dapr dependency is restored properly and that the project compiles. From the VS Code Terminal tab, open the developer command prompt or PowerShell terminal and navigate to the parent directory that hosts the .csproj project folder and build the project.

```
cd ~/BenefitsManager.Backend.Bff.Api
dotnet build
```

Now you are ready to run both applications and debug them. You can store new claims, update them, delete existing claims, and mark them as completed. The data should be stored in your local Redis instance.

4.11 Use Azure Cosmos DB with Dapr State Store Management API

4.11.1 Provision Cosmos DB Resources

In this section, let's create an Azure Cosmos DB account, database, and a new container that will store our claims. You can use the PowerShell script below to create the Cosmos DB resources on the same resource group we

CHAPTER 4   INTEGRATING DAPR WITH AZURE CONTAINER APPS

used in the previous chapters. You need to set the variable name of the $COSMOS_DB_ACCOUNT to a unique name as it needs to be unique globally. Remember to replace the placeholders with your own values:

```
$AZURE_SUBSCRIPTION_ID = az account show --query id
--output tsv

# Create a random, 4-digit, Azure safe string
$RANDOM_STRING=-join ((97..122) + (48..57) | Get-Random -Count 4
| ForEach-Object { [char]$_ })
$RESOURCE_GROUP="rg-benefits-manager"
$LOCATION="eastus"

$COSMOS_DB_ACCOUNT="cosmos-claims-tracker-state-store-
$RANDOM_STRING"
$COSMOS_DB_DBNAME="claimsmanagerdb"
$COSMOS_DB_CONTAINER="claimscollection"

# Check if Cosmos account name already exists globally
$result = az cosmosdb check-name-exists `
--name $COSMOS_DB_ACCOUNT

# Continue if the Cosmos DB account does not yet exist
if ($result -eq "false") {
    echo "Creating Cosmos DB account..."

    # Create a Cosmos account for SQL API
    az cosmosdb create `
    --name $COSMOS_DB_ACCOUNT `
    --resource-group $RESOURCE_GROUP

    # Create a SQL API database
    az cosmosdb sql database create `
    --name $COSMOS_DB_DBNAME `
    --resource-group $RESOURCE_GROUP `
```

```
    --account-name $COSMOS_DB_ACCOUNT

    # Create a SQL API container
    az cosmosdb sql container create `
    --name $COSMOS_DB_CONTAINER `
    --resource-group $RESOURCE_GROUP `
    --account-name $COSMOS_DB_ACCOUNT `
    --database-name $COSMOS_DB_DBNAME `
    --partition-key-path "/id" `
    --throughput 400

    $COSMOS_DB_ENDPOINT=(az cosmosdb show `
    --name $COSMOS_DB_ACCOUNT `
    --resource-group $RESOURCE_GROUP `
    --query documentEndpoint `
    --output tsv)

    echo "Cosmos DB Endpoint: "
    echo $COSMOS_DB_ENDPOINT
}
```

It will take three to four minutes to create all the resources as shown in Figure 4-13 before printing out the Cosmos DB endpoint in the console output as shown in Figure 4-14.

CHAPTER 4 INTEGRATING DAPR WITH AZURE CONTAINER APPS

```
PS C:\WINDOWS\system32> # Check if Cosmos account name already exists globally
>> $result = az cosmosdb check-name-exists `
>> --name $COSMOS_DB_ACCOUNT
>>
>> # Continue if the Cosmos DB account does not yet exist
>> if ($result -eq "false") {
>>     echo "Creating Cosmos DB account..."
>>
>>     # Create a Cosmos account for SQL API
>>     az cosmosdb create `
>>     --name $COSMOS_DB_ACCOUNT `
>>     --resource-group $RESOURCE_GROUP
>>
>>     # Create a SQL API database
>>     az cosmosdb sql database create `
>>     --name $COSMOS_DB_DBNAME `
>>     --resource-group $RESOURCE_GROUP `
>>     --account-name $COSMOS_DB_ACCOUNT
>>
>>     # Create a SQL API container
>>     az cosmosdb sql container create `
>>     --name $COSMOS_DB_CONTAINER `
>>     --resource-group $RESOURCE_GROUP `
>>     --account-name $COSMOS_DB_ACCOUNT `
>>     --database-name $COSMOS_DB_DBNAME `
>>     --partition-key-path "/id" `
>>     --throughput 400
>>
>>     $COSMOS_DB_ENDPOINT=(az cosmosdb show `
>>     --name $COSMOS_DB_ACCOUNT `
>>     --resource-group $RESOURCE_GROUP `
>>     --query documentEndpoint `
>>     --output tsv)
>>
>>     echo "Cosmos DB Endpoint: "
>>     echo $COSMOS_DB_ENDPOINT
>> }
Creating Cosmos DB account...
```

Figure 4-13. Executing PowerShell commands to create Cosmos DB-related resources

CHAPTER 4 INTEGRATING DAPR WITH AZURE CONTAINER APPS

```
      }
    ],
    "ts": 1733615355.0,
    "uniqueKeyPolicy": {
      "uniqueKeys": []
    }
  },
  "resourceGroup": "rg-benefits-manager",
  "tags": null,
  "type": "Microsoft.DocumentDB/databaseAccounts/sqlDatabases/containers"
}
Cosmos DB Endpoint:
https://cosmos-claims-tracker-state-store-z3ui.documents.azure.com:443/
PS C:\WINDOWS\system32>
```

Figure 4-14. Cosmos DB endpoint is printed after resources are created.

POINT TO NOTE

The **PrimaryMasterKey** connection string is required solely for local testing on the development machine. When deploying the Dapr component to the Azure Container Apps environment, we will use a different approach, specifically managed identities.

Once the script's execution is completed, we need to get the primaryMasterKey of the Cosmos DB account next. You can do this using the PowerShell script below. Copy the value of primaryMasterKey as we will use it in the next step.

```
# List Azure Cosmos DB keys
$COSMOS_DB_PRIMARY_MASTER_KEY=(az cosmosdb keys list `
--name $COSMOS_DB_ACCOUNT `
--resource-group $RESOURCE_GROUP `
--query primaryMasterKey `
--output tsv)
```

```
echo "Cosmos DB Primary Master Key:"
echo $COSMOS_DB_PRIMARY_MASTER_KEY
```

4.11.2 Create a Component File for State Store Management

Dapr uses a modular design where functionality is delivered as a component. Each component has an interface definition. All the components are pluggable so that you can swap out one component with the same interface for another.

Components are configured at design-time with a YAML file, which is stored in either a components/local folder within your solution or globally in the *.dapr* folder created when invoking **dapr init**. These YAML files adhere to the generic Dapr component schema, but each is specific to the component specification.

It is important to understand that the component spec values, particularly the spec *metadata*, can change between components of the same component type. As a result, it is strongly recommended to review a component's specs, paying particular attention to the sample payloads for requests to set the metadata used to interact with the component.

The diagram in Figure 4-15, sourced from the official Dapr documentation, illustrates examples of components for each component type. Our focus now is on the State Stores components, specifically the one for Azure Cosmos DB.

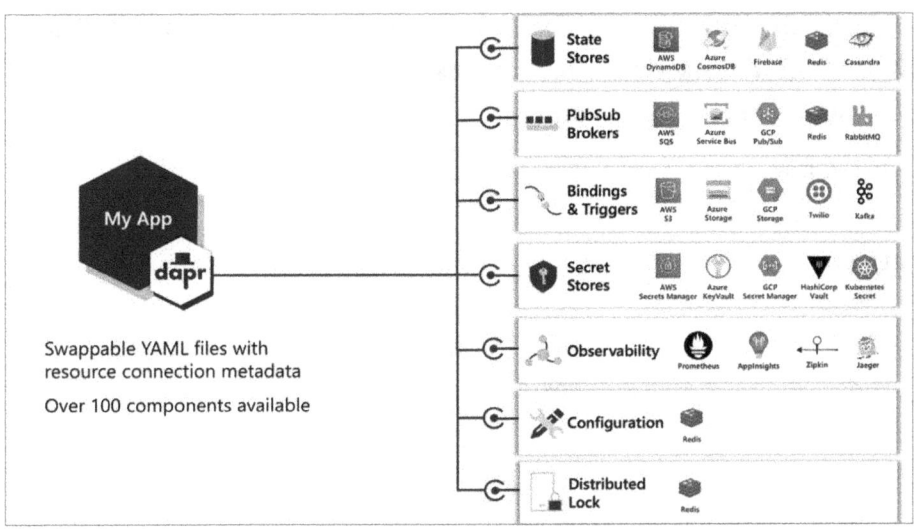

Figure 4-15. *List of components Dapr supports*

To add the component file state store, add a new folder named components under the solution root directory and add a new YAML file as shown below. The values for URL and masterKey can be found in the console output from the most recently executed commands during provisioning Cosmos DB.

POINT TO NOTE
You need to replace the **masterKey** value with your Cosmos Account key. Remember this is only needed for local development debugging; we will not be using the masterKey when we deploy to ACA.

Replace the **URL** value with the **URI** value of your Azure Cosmos DB account. You can get that from the Azure portal by navigating to the Azure Cosmos DB account overview page and get the URI value from there.

CHAPTER 4   INTEGRATING DAPR WITH AZURE CONTAINER APPS

Basically, the URI should have the following structure: **https://COSMOS_DB_ACCOUNT.documents.azure.com:443/**

dapr-statestore-cosmos.yaml

```
apiVersion: dapr.io/v1alpha1
kind: Component
metadata:
  name: statestore
spec:
  type: state.azure.cosmosdb
  version: v1
  metadata:
  - name: url
    value: https://cosmos-claims-tracker-state-store-z3ui.
    documents.azure.com:443/
  - name: masterKey
    value: "<value of master key>"
  - name: database
    value: claimsmanagerdb
  - name: collection
    value: claimscollection
scopes:
- BenefitsManager-Backend-Bff-Api
```

Quick overview of **dapr-statestore-cosmos.yaml** file contents:

- The name `statestore` that should match the name of state store we've used in the `ClaimsStoreManager.cs` file. As well, we have set the metadata key/value to allow us to connect to Azure Cosmos DB.

CHAPTER 4   INTEGRATING DAPR WITH AZURE CONTAINER APPS

- We've updated the other metadata keys such as `database`, `collection`, etc., to match the values of your Cosmos DB instance. For full metadata specs, you can check this link: https://docs.dapr.io/reference/components-reference/supported-state-stores/setup-azure-cosmosdb/.

- By default, all Dapr-enabled container apps within the same environment will load the full set of deployed components. By adding `scopes` to a component, you tell the Dapr sidecars for each respective container app which components to load at runtime. Using scopes is recommended for production workloads. In our case, we have set the scopes to `BenefitsManager-Backend-Bff-Api`, which represents the dapr-app-id that is associated to the container app that needs access to Azure Cosmos DB State Store as this will be the application that needs access to Azure Cosmos DB State Store.

POINT TO NOTE

Dapr component scopes correspond to the Dapr application ID of a container app, not the container app name.

4.11.3 Running Backend and Frontend Application

Now you should be ready to launch both applications and start doing CRUD operations from the frontend web app including querying the store. All your data will be stored in the Cosmos DB Database you just provisioned.

If you have been running different microservices using the **debug and launch Dapr applications in VS Code** (refer to Section 4.8), then remember to uncomment the following line inside the tasks.json file. This will instruct Dapr to load the local projects components located at ./components instead of the global components' folder.

```
{
    "componentsPath": "./components"
}
```

If you have been using the Dapr CLI commands instead of the aforementioned debugging, then you will need to execute the backend API with the resources-path property as follows:

```
Cd ~/BenefitsManager.Backend.BFF.API
dapr run `
--app-id BenefitsManager-Backend-Bff-Api `
--app-port $API_APP_PORT `
--dapr-http-port 3500 `
--app-ssl `
--resources-path "../components" `
-- dotnet run --launch-profile https
```

After creating a new claim record from the Web UI, you can navigate to the Data Explorer on the Azure portal (https://portal.azure.com) for the Azure Cosmos DB account. It should be like Figure 4-16.

CHAPTER 4   INTEGRATING DAPR WITH AZURE CONTAINER APPS

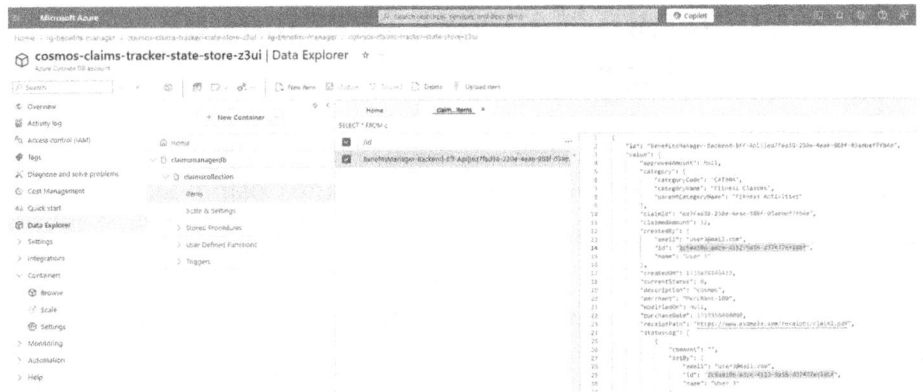

Figure 4-16. *Cosmos DB Data Explorer to see the uploaded claim record inside collection*

When you look at the key stored per entry and, for example, **BenefitsManager-Backend-Bff-Api**||**ed7fad38-230e-4eae-988f-03aebef7f b4e**, you will notice that the key is prefixed with the Dapr application App Id responsible to store this entry, which, in our case, is **BenefitsManager-Backend-Bff-Api**. There might be some scenarios in which you need to have another service to access the same data store (not recommended as each service should be responsible for its own data store), in which case you can change the default behavior.

This can be done by adding the meta tag below to the component file. For example, if we need to set the value of the prefix to a constant value such as ClaimId, we can do the following:

```
spec:
    metadata:
    - name: keyPrefix
    - value: ClaimId
```

If we need to totally omit the key prefix, so it is accessed across multiple Dapr applications, we can set the value to none.

135

4.11.4 Configure Managed Identities in Container App

As mentioned earlier, we will not use connection strings to establish the connection between our Container App and Azure Cosmos DB when deploying to Azure Container Apps (ACA).

Cosmos DB Master Key/Connection string was only used when debugging locally. Now we will rely on Managed Identities to allow our container app to access Cosmos DB. With Managed Identities, you don't worry about storing the keys securely and rotate them inside your application. This approach is safer and easier to manage.

We will be using a system-assigned identity with a role assignment to grant our backend API container app permissions to access data stored in Cosmos DB. We need to assign it a custom role for the Cosmos DB data plane. In this example, we are going to use a built-in role, named **Cosmos DB Built-in Data Contributor**, which grants our application full read-write access to the data. You can optionally create custom, fine-tuned roles following the instructions in the official docs (https://learn.microsoft.com/en-us/azure/cosmos-db/nosql/security/how-to-grant-data-plane-role-based-access?tabs=built-in-definition%2Ccsharp&pivots=azure-interface-cli).

```
$BE_BFF_API_NAME="ca-benefitsmanager-bff-api"
$COSMOS_DB_ACCOUNT="cosmos-claims-tracker-state-store-z3ui"
$RESOURCE_GROUP="rg-benefits-manager"

az containerapp identity assign `
--name $BE_BFF_API_NAME `
--resource-group $RESOURCE_GROUP `
--system-assigned

$COSMOS_DB_PRIMARY_MASTER_KEY=(az cosmosdb keys list `
--name $COSMOS_DB_ACCOUNT `
```

CHAPTER 4 INTEGRATING DAPR WITH AZURE CONTAINER APPS

```
--resource-group $RESOURCE_GROUP `
--query primaryMasterKey `
--output tsv)

$BACKEND_API_PRINCIPAL_ID=(az containerapp identity show `
--name $BE_BFF_API_NAME `
--resource-group $RESOURCE_GROUP `
--query principalId `
--output tsv)
```

This command will create an Enterprise Application (basically a Service Principal) within Azure AD, which is linked to our container app. The output of this command will be similar to the one shown below. Keep a note of the property principalId as we are going to use it in the next step.

```
{
    "principalId": "[your principal id will be
    displayed here]",
    "tenantId": "[your tenant id will be displayed here]",
    "type": "SystemAssigned"
}
```

4.11.5 Assign the Container App System-Identity to the Built-in Cosmos DB Role

We need to associate the container app system-identity with the target Cosmos DB resource. You can read more about Azure built-in roles for Cosmos DB or how to create custom, fine-tuned roles (refer to https://learn.microsoft.com/en-us/azure/cosmos-db/nosql/security/how-to-grant-data-plane-role-based-access?tabs=built-in-definition%2Ccsharp&pivots=azure-interface-cli#built-in-role-definitions). Run the command below to associate the container app system-assigned identity with the Cosmos DB Built-in Data Contributor role.

```
$ROLE_ID = "00000000-0000-0000-0000-000000000002" #"Cosmos DB
Built-in Data Contributor"

az cosmosdb sql role assignment create `
--resource-group $RESOURCE_GROUP `
--account-name $COSMOS_DB_ACCOUNT `
--scope "/" `
--principal-id $BACKEND_API_PRINCIPAL_ID `
--role-definition-id $ROLE_ID
```

4.12 Deploy Backend API and Frontend Web App Projects to ACA

We are almost ready to deploy all local changes from this chapter and the previous chapter to ACA. But before we do that, we need one last addition.

We have to create a **Dapr component schema file** for Azure Cosmos DB that meets the specs defined by Azure Container Apps. The reason for this variance is that ACA Dapr schema is slightly simplified to support Dapr components and removes unnecessary fields, including apiVersion, kind, and redundant metadata and spec properties.

4.12.1 Create an ACA-Dapr Component File for State Store Management

The general recommendation is to separate the component files used for deployment to Azure Container Apps from those used for running the application locally in a self-hosted Dapr environment.

Create a new folder named **aca-components** under the parent root directory ClaimsTracker.ContainerApps, and then add a new file as shown below:

Containerapps-statestore-cosmos.yaml

```
componentType: state.azure.cosmosdb
version: v1
metadata:
  - name: url
    value: https://cosmos-claims-tracker-state-store-z3ui.
    documents.azure.com:443/
  - name: database
    value: claimsmanagerdb
  - name: collection
    value: claimscollection
scopes:
  - ca-benefitsmanager-bff-api
```

4.12.2 Build Frontend Web App and Backend API App Images in Azure Container Registry

We need to build and deploy both app images to ACR, so they are ready to be deployed to Azure Container Apps. To do so, continue using the same PowerShell console and paste the code below. Ensure you are in the root directory (refer to Chapters 2 and 3 as we have done previously).

```
$BE_BFF_API_NAME="ca-benefitsmanager-bff-api"
$AZURE_CONTAINER_REGISTRY_NAME="crbenefitsmanagerz4l6"

az acr build `
--registry $AZURE_CONTAINER_REGISTRY_NAME `
--image "benefitsmanager/$BE_BFF_API_NAME" `
--file 'BenefitsManager.Backend.Bff.Api/Dockerfile' .
```

```
$FE_WEB_UI_NAME = "ca-benefitsmanager-fe-ui"
az acr build `
--registry $AZURE_CONTAINER_REGISTRY_NAME `
--image "benefitsmanager/$FE_WEB_UI_NAME" `
--file 'BenefitsManager.Frontend.WebPortal.Ui/Dockerfile' .
```

4.12.3 Add Cosmos DB Dapr State Store to the Azure Container Apps Environment

We need to run the command below to add the YAML file .\aca-components\containerapps-statestore-cosmos.yaml to the Azure Container Apps environment.

```
$ENVIRONMENT="cae-benefits-manager"
$RESOURCE_GROUP="rg-benefits-manager"

az containerapp env dapr-component set `
--name $ENVIRONMENT `
--resource-group $RESOURCE_GROUP `
--dapr-component-name statestore `
--yaml '.\aca-components\containerapps-statestore-cosmos.yaml'
```

4.12.4 Enable Dapr for Both Frontend and Backend Container Apps

Enable Dapr for both container apps by running the two commands below in the PowerShell console.

```
az containerapp dapr enable `
--name $BE_BFF_API_NAME `
--resource-group $RESOURCE_GROUP `
--dapr-app-id $BE_BFF_API_NAME `
--dapr-app-port $TARGET_PORT
```

```
az containerapp dapr enable `
--name $FE_WEB_UI_NAME `
--resource-group $RESOURCE_GROUP `
--dapr-app-id  $FE_WEB_UI_NAME `
--dapr-app-port $TARGET_PORT
```

4.12.5 Deploy New Revisions of Both Frontend and Backend Apps to ACA

Run the commands below to update both container apps and deploy the new images from ACR.

```
# Update Frontend web app container app and create a new revision
az containerapp update `
 --name $FE_WEB_UI_NAME  `
--resource-group $RESOURCE_GROUP  `
--revision-suffix v$TODAY

# Update Backend API App container app and create a new revision
az containerapp update `
--name $BE_BFF_API_NAME `
 --resource-group $RESOURCE_GROUP  `
--revision-suffix v$TODAY-1
```

4.13 Summary

In this chapter, we introduced Dapr, its benefits, and a step-by-step guide to configuring Dapr on a local machine. We covered Dapr building blocks, with a focus on state stores, and explored how to use the Dapr State Store SDK and integrate it into the code base. Additionally, we learned how to configure VS Code to run and debug multiple Dapr applications simultaneously, eliminating the need to open multiple PowerShell windows.

Finally, we concluded by provisioning Azure Cosmos DB as a state store instead of using in-memory storage and demonstrated how to enable Dapr for both frontend and backend applications running in Azure Container Apps (ACA).

In Chapter 5, we will delve into the Dapr publisher/subscriber pattern and explore asynchronous communication using the Dapr Pub/Sub API.

CHAPTER 5

Async Communication with Dapr Pub/Sub API

In this chapter, you will explore the Dapr Pub/Sub pattern, focusing on its integration with Azure Container Apps. The learning objectives for this chapter include

- Introduction to the Dapr Pub/Sub pattern.
- Testing the Pub/Sub pattern locally.
- Introduce new background service, ACA Processor – Backend, configured for Dapr.
- Use Azure Service Bus as a service broker for Dapr Pub/Sub API.
- Deploy background service to Azure Container Apps.

5.1 Pub/Sub Pattern with Dapr

As a best practice, it is recommended that we decouple services from each other. A conventional way to do so is by employing the Publisher-Subscriber (Pub/Sub) pattern. The primary advantage of this pattern is

CHAPTER 5   ASYNC COMMUNICATION WITH DAPR PUB/SUB API

that it offers loose coupling between services where the sender/publisher of the message doesn't know anything about the receivers/consumers. This can be done in a 1-1 or 1-many constellation in which multiple consumers each receive a copy of the message in a totally different way. For example, imagine adding another consumer who is responsible for sending push notifications to the Claim owner (e.g., if we had a mobile app channel).

In Chapter 4, we explored how to decouple the ACA Web - Frontend from the ACA API Backend using asynchronous HTTP calls via Dapr. We also covered integrating Redis cache locally and Azure Cosmos DB in the cloud.

In this chapter, we will set up a Pub/Sub pattern to enable asynchronous messaging between microservices. This publisher-subscriber model relies on a message broker, which handles receiving messages from the publisher, storing them for durability, and delivering them to interested consumers for processing. Consumers do not need to be available when the message is stored in the broker; they can retrieve and process messages asynchronously at a later time. High-level overview of how the Pub/Sub pattern works is shown in Figure 5-1.

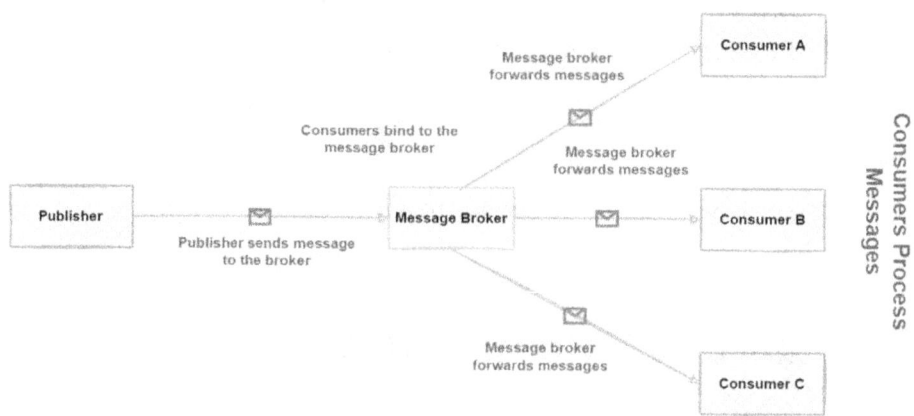

Figure 5-1. High-level overview of the Pub/Sub pattern

CHAPTER 5   ASYNC COMMUNICATION WITH DAPR PUB/SUB API

If you implemented the Pub/Sub pattern before, you already know that there is a lot of plumbing needed on the publisher and subscriber components to publish and consume messages. In addition, each message broker has its own SDK and implementation. So, you need to write your code in an abstracted way to hide the specific implementation details for each message broker SDK and make it easier for the publisher and consumers to reuse this functionality. Dapr provides a building block that streamlines the implementation of Pub/Sub functionality by decoupling the underlying provider from how the pattern is used within the application. This abstraction ensures that the application remains unaware of its communication counterpart, which is intentional and beneficial for maintaining application portability and immutability.

Simply put, the Dapr Pub/Sub building block offers a platform-agnostic API framework for sending and receiving messages. Producer services publish messages to a specific topic, while consumer services subscribe to that topic to receive and process them.

5.2 Testing Pub/Sub Locally

To try this out, we can directly invoke the Pub/Sub API and publish a message to Redis locally. If you remember from Chapter 4, when we initialized Dapr in a local development environment, it installed the Redis container instance locally. Therefore, we can use Redis locally to publish and subscribe to a topic. If you navigate to the path %USERPROFILE%\.dapr\components (assuming you are using Windows), you will find a file named pubsub.yaml. Inside this file, you will see the properties needed to access the local Redis instance. The publisher/subscriber brokers template component file structure can be found here.

CHAPTER 5   ASYNC COMMUNICATION WITH DAPR PUB/SUB API

However, we want to have more control and provide our own component file, so let's create a Pub/Sub component file in our components folder as shown below:

```
apiVersion: dapr.io/v1alpha1
kind: Component
metadata:
  name: claimspubsub
spec:
  type: pubsub.redis
  version: v1
  metadata:
    - name: redisHost
      value: localhost:6379
    - name: redisPassword
      value: ""
```

To try out the Pub/Sub API, run the backend API from VS Code by running the command below:

```
Cd ~/BenefitsManager.Backend.BFF.API

dapr run `
--app-id BenefitsManager-Backend-Bff-Api `
--app-port $API_APP_PORT `
--dapr-http-port 3500 `
--app-ssl `
--resources-path "../components" `
-- dotnet run --launch-profile https
```

Let's try to publish a message by sending a POST request to http://localhost:3500/v1.0/publish/claimspubsub/claimsavedtopic. Here's how the URL is structured:

CHAPTER 5   ASYNC COMMUNICATION WITH DAPR PUB/SUB API

- **http://localhost:3500**: This is the Dapr sidecar endpoint running on your local machine, listening on port 3500.

- **/v1.0**: This specifies the API version (v1.0) of Dapr.

- **/publish**: This is the Dapr API method used to publish messages to a Pub/Sub component.

- **/claimspubsub**: This is the name of the Pub/Sub component (configured in the Dapr setup, e.g., Redis, Kafka, Azure Service Bus).

- **/claimsavedtopic**: This is the topic name to which the message will be published.

Don't forget to set the **Content-Type** header to **application/json** when sending the request body as below:

```
{
    "claimId": "59E029B1-1621-45A1-8263-A77AA7758FAE",
    "merchant": "Merchant-10",
    "claimedAmount": 80,
    "approvedAmount": null,
    "purchaseDate": 1733201907427,
    "category": {
      "categoryCode": "CAT004",
      "parentCategoryName": "Fitness Activities",
      "categoryName": "Gym"
    },
    "description": "Random description2",
    "statusLog": [
      {
        "status": 0,
        "comment": "",
```

147

```
            "setBy": {
              "id": "323a3afe-711f-4aa6-80d0-f848d24a5340",
              "email": "user3@mail.com",
              "name": "User-3"
            },
            "ts": 1733450307427
          }
        ],
        "currentStatus": 0,
        "receiptPath": "https://storage.blob.core.windows.net/
        claims/63105a50-e295-4619-8708-c790601c976d/receipt.pdf",
        "createdBy": {
          "id": "323a3afe-711f-4aa6-80d0-f848d24a5340",
          "email": "user3@mail.com",
          "name": "User-3"
        },
        "createdOn": 1733450307427,
        "modifiedOn": null
}
```

A **No Content** response from this endpoint indicates that the service broker (Redis) has successfully published the message to the **claimsavedtopic** as shown in figure 5-2.

CHAPTER 5   ASYNC COMMUNICATION WITH DAPR PUB/SUB API

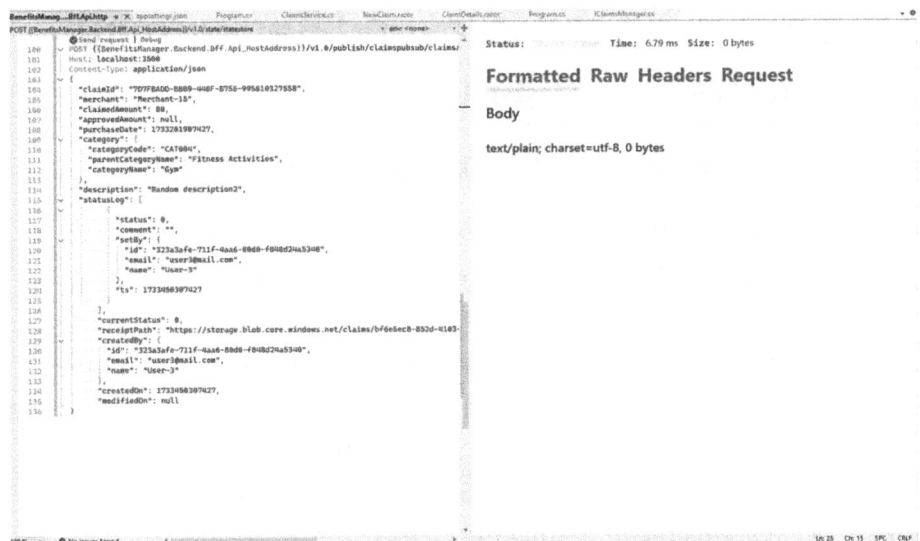

Figure 5-2. *Sending HTTP request to state store API endpoint, which returns 204 status*

You can also verify that the topic was created successfully by using the Redis Xplorer extension in VS Code, as illustrated in Figure 5-3.

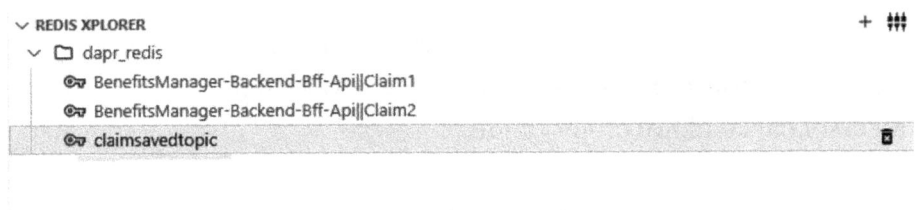

Figure 5-3. *Redis Xplorer, displaying claimsavedtopic*

Currently, the published messages are sitting idle in the message broker topic. We don't have any subscribers connected to the service broker on the **claimsavedtopic** that are interested in consuming and processing these messages. In the next section, we will set up a consumer to handle this.

149

CHAPTER 5　ASYNC COMMUNICATION WITH DAPR PUB/SUB API

5.3 Setting Up the Backend Background Processor Project

5.3.1 Create the Backend Service Project

In this section, we will create a new background service named "ACA Processor – Backend," which was mentioned in our architecture diagram (refer to Chapter 1). This new service will be responsible for sending emails to expense owners based on messages received from an Azure Service Bus Topic when there are changes in the expense status. We can do this in the backend API and send the email right after saving the claim, but we want to offload this process to another service and keep the backend API service responsible for managing claims data only.

Now we will add a new ASP.NET Core Web API project named **BenefitsManager.Processor.Backend.Svc**. Open a command-line terminal and navigate to the root folder.

```
dotnet new webapi --use-controllers -o BenefitsManager.Processor.Backend.Svc
```

Delete the boilerplate WeatherForecast.cs and Controllers\WeatherForecastController.cs files from the new BenefitsClaimManager.Processor.Backend.Svc project folder.

5.3.2 Docker Configuration

To deploy the BenefitsManager.Processor.Backend.Svc application to Azure Container Apps, we need to containerize this application and push the container image to Azure Container Registry.

Open the VS Code Command Palette (Ctrl+Shift+P) and select Docker: Add Docker Files to Workspace.

- Use .NET:ASP.NET Core when prompted for the application platform.
- Choose the newly created project, if prompted.
- Choose Linux when prompted to choose the operating system.
- Set the application port to 8080.
- You will be asked if you want to add Docker Compose files. Select No.
- Dockerfile and .dockerignore files are added to the workspace.

Open Dockerfile and replace

FROM --platform=$BUILDPLATFORM mcr.microsoft.com/dotnet/sdk:9.0 AS build

with

FROM mcr.microsoft.com/dotnet/sdk:9.0 AS build

POINT TO NOTE

Azure Container Registry does not set $BUILDPLATFORM presently when building containers. This consequently causes the build to fail. See https://github.com/microsoft/vscode-docker/issues/4149 for details. Therefore, we removed it from the file as a workaround mentioned by the product team.

```
FROM mcr.microsoft.com/dotnet/aspnet:9.0 AS base
USER $APP_UID
WORKDIR /app
EXPOSE 8080
EXPOSE 8081

# This stage is used to build the service project
FROM mcr.microsoft.com/dotnet/sdk:9.0 AS build
ARG BUILD_CONFIGURATION=Release
WORKDIR /src
COPY ["BenefitsManager.Processor.Backend.Svc/BenefitsManager.Processor.Backend.Svc.csproj", "BenefitsManager.Processor.Backend.Svc/"]
RUN dotnet restore "./BenefitsManager.Processor.Backend.Svc/BenefitsManager.Processor.Backend.Svc.csproj"
COPY . .
WORKDIR "/src/BenefitsManager.Processor.Backend.Svc"
RUN dotnet build "./BenefitsManager.Processor.Backend.Svc.csproj" -c $BUILD_CONFIGURATION -o /app/build

# This stage is used to publish the service project to be copied to the final stage
FROM build AS publish
ARG BUILD_CONFIGURATION=Release
RUN dotnet publish "./BenefitsManager.Processor.Backend.Svc.csproj" -c $BUILD_CONFIGURATION -o /app/publish /p:UseAppHost=false

# This stage is used in production or when running from VS in regular mode (Default when not using the Debug configuration)
FROM base AS final
WORKDIR /app
```

```
COPY --from=publish /app/publish .
ENTRYPOINT ["dotnet", "BenefitsManager.Processor.Backend.
Svc.dll"]
```

5.3.3 Add Models

As mentioned in Chapter 3, we will be creating a common library to move the model classes into it. You can add it directly from Visual Studio or from a command line. Open a command-line terminal and navigate to the root folder.

```
dotnet new classlib -n BenefitsManager.Common.Models
```

Move ClaimModel.cs, IClaimsManager.cs, and ClaimStatus.cs into the newly created common library and delete these model classes from both Backend and Frontend projects. Once done, add **BenefitsManager.Common.Models** as project reference to both Backend and Frontend projects. Update all the namespace references in the project and make sure to rebuild the entire solution.

To avoid duplication, we are not displaying ClaimModel class contents; refer to Chapter 2 to see the file contents.

5.3.4 Install the Dapr SDK Client NuGet Package

To enable subscription to the service broker topic programmatically, we will install the Dapr SDK into the **BenefitsManager.Processor.Backend.Svc** project. Add the highlighted NuGet package to the **BenefitsManager.Processor.Backend.Svc.csproj** file as shown below:

```
<PackageReference Include="Dapr.AspNetCore" Version="1.14.0" />
```

Reference common library BenefitsManager.Common.Models as project reference to bring in the models.

5.3.5 Create an API Endpoint for the Consumer to Subscribe to the Topic

Let's create an endpoint that will be responsible for subscribing to the topic in the message broker we are interested in. This endpoint will start receiving the message published from the backend API producer. Add a new controller under the Controllers folder.

```csharp
using Dapr.Client;
using BenefitsManager.Common.Models;
using Microsoft.AspNetCore.Mvc;
using Dapr;

namespace BenefitsManager.Processor.Backend.Svc.Controllers
{
    [Route("api/claimsnotifier")]
    [ApiController]
    public class ClaimsNotifierController : ControllerBase
    {
        private readonly IConfiguration _config;
        private readonly ILogger _logger;
        private readonly DaprClient _daprClient;

        public ClaimsNotifierController(IConfiguration config,
        ILogger<ClaimsNotifierController> logger, DaprClient
        daprClient)
        {
            _config = config;
            _logger = logger;
            _daprClient = daprClient;
        }
```

CHAPTER 5 ASYNC COMMUNICATION WITH DAPR PUB/SUB API

```
[Topic("dapr-pubsub-servicebus",
"claimsavedtopic")]    // Dapr Pub Sub Service Bus
[Topic("claimspubsub",
"claimsavedtopic")]               // Redis
[HttpPost("claimsaved")]
public IActionResult ClaimSaved([FromBody] ClaimModel
claimModel)
{
    const string ClaimsMessage = "Started processing
    message with Claim Id '{0}'";
    var msg = string.Format(ClaimsMessage, claimModel.
    ClaimId);
    _logger.LogInformation(ClaimsMessage, claimModel.
    ClaimId);

    return Ok(msg);
    }
  }
}
```

You may be wondering how the consumer was able to identify what are the subscriptions available and on which route they can be found at. The answer for this is that at startup on the consumer service (more on that below after we add app.MapSubscribeHandler()), the Dapr runtime will call the application on a well-known endpoint to identify and create the required subscriptions.

The well-known endpoint can be reached on this endpoint: http://localhost:<appPort>/dapr/subscribe. When you invoke this endpoint, the response will contain an array of all available topics for which the applications will subscribe. Each includes a route to call when the topic receives a message. This was generated as we used the attribute Dapr.Topic on the action method api/claimsnotifier/claimsaved.

CHAPTER 5   ASYNC COMMUNICATION WITH DAPR PUB/SUB API

In the case of our BenefitsManager application, the URL becomes http://localhost:3500/dapr/subscribe; a sample response will be as follows:

```
[
    {
    "pubsubname": "claimspubsub",
    "topic": "claimsavedtopic",
    "route": "/api/claimsnotifier/claimsaved"
    }
]
```

That means when a message is published on the PubSubname claimspubsub on the topic claimsavedtopic, it will be routed to the action method /api/claimsnotifier/claimsaved and will be consumed in this action method.

The main advantage with the Pub-Sub pattern is loose coupling, where it decouples services that send messages(publishers) to those that receive messages(consumers). Figure 5-4 shows a high-level architecture of the Pub/Sub pattern.

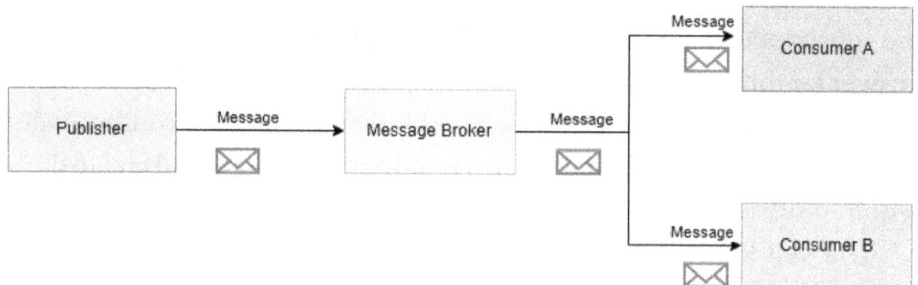

Figure 5-4. *Pub/Sub high-level architecture*

156

5.3.6 Register Dapr and Subscribe Handler at the Consumer Startup

Open the Program.cs file inside the BenefitsManager.Processor.Backend. Svc project to update as shown below:

```
namespace BenefitsManager.Processor.Backend.Svc
{
    public class Program
    {
        public static void Main(string[] args)
        {
            var builder = WebApplication.CreateBuilder(args);

            // Add services to the container.

            builder.Services.AddControllers().AddDapr();

            builder.Services.AddControllers();
            // Learn more about configuring Swagger/OpenAPI at https://aka.ms/aspnetcore/swashbuckle
            builder.Services.AddEndpointsApiExplorer();
            builder.Services.AddSwaggerGen();

            var app = builder.Build();

            // Configure the HTTP request pipeline.
            if (app.Environment.IsDevelopment())
            {
                app.UseSwagger();
                app.UseSwaggerUI();
            }
```

```
            app.UseHttpsRedirection();

            app.UseAuthorization();

            app.UseCloudEvents();

            app.MapControllers();

            app.MapSubscribeHandler();

            app.Run();
        }
    }
}
```

Curious about the lines of code above? Let's discuss them one by one.

- The line **builder.Services.AddControllers(). AddDapr();**. The extension method **AddDapr** registers the necessary services to integrate Dapr into the MVC pipeline. It also registers a DaprClient instance into the dependency injection container, which then can be injected anywhere into your service. We will see how we are injecting DaprClient in the controller constructor later on.

- The line **app.UseCloudEvents();**. The extension method **UseCloudEvents** adds CloudEvents middleware into the ASP.NET Core middleware pipeline. This middleware will unwrap requests that use the CloudEvents structured format, so the receiving method can read the event payload directly. You can read more about CloudEvents at https://cloudevents.io/, which includes specs for describing event data in a common and standard way.

CHAPTER 5   ASYNC COMMUNICATION WITH DAPR PUB/SUB API

- The line **app.MapSubscribeHandler();**. We make the endpoint **http://localhost:<appPort>/dapr/subscribe** available for the consumer so it responds and returns available subscriptions. When this endpoint is called, it will automatically find all WebAPI action methods decorated with the Dapr.Topic attribute and instruct Dapr to create subscriptions for them.

Let's verify that the Dapr dependency is restored properly and that the project compiles. From the VS Code Terminal tab, open the developer command prompt or PowerShell terminal and navigate to the parent directory that hosts the .csproj project folder and build the project as shown in Figure 5-5.

```
Cd ~/BenefitsManager.Processor.Backend.Svc
dotnet build
```

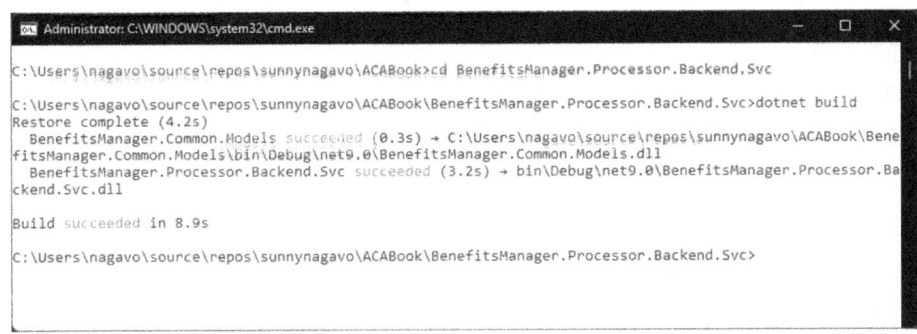

Figure 5-5. *Compiling backend processor project*

With all the code ready in place, we are ready to run the publisher service **Backend API** and the consumer service **Backend Background Service** and test the Pub/Sub pattern end to end.

Open two separate PowerShell console windows and ensure you are on the right root folder of each respective project.

CHAPTER 5   ASYNC COMMUNICATION WITH DAPR PUB/SUB API

To run the Backend API project:

```
Cd ~/BenefitsManager.Backend.BFF.API
```

```
dapr run `
--app-id BenefitsManager-Backend-Bff-Api `
--app-port $API_APP_PORT `
--dapr-http-port 3500 `
--app-ssl `
--scheduler-host-address "" `
--resources-path "../components" `
-- dotnet run --launch-profile https
```

To run the Backend Background Service project:

```
Cd ~/BenefitsManager.Processor.Backend.Svc
$BACKEND_SERVICE_APP_PORT = <backend service https port in Properties->launchSettings.json (e.g. 7148)>
```

```
dapr run `
--app-id BenefitsManager-Backend-Processor `
--app-port $BACKEND_SERVICE_APP_PORT `
--dapr-http-port 3502 `
--app-ssl `
--scheduler-host-address "" `
--resources-path "../components" `
-- dotnet run --launch-profile https
```

Now let's try to publish a message by sending a POST request to http://localhost:3500/v1.0/publish/**claimspubsub**/claimsavedtopic with the following request body. Don't forget to set the Content-Type header to application/json.

```
POST /v1.0/publish/claimspubsub/claimsavedtopic HTTP/1.1
Host: localhost:3500
Content-Type: application/json
```

```json
{
  "claimId": "59E029B1-1621-45A1-8263-A77AA7758FAE",
  "merchant": "Merchant-10",
  "claimedAmount": 80,
  "approvedAmount": null,
  "purchaseDate": 1733201907427,
  "category": {
    "categoryCode": "CAT004",
    "parentCategoryName": "Fitness Activities",
    "categoryName": "Gym"
  },
  "description": "Random description2",
  "statusLog": [
    {
      "status": 0,
      "comment": "",
      "setBy": {
        "id": "323a3afe-711f-4aa6-80d0-f848d24a5340",
        "email": "user3@mail.com",
        "name": "User-3"
      },
      "ts": 1733450307427
    }
  ],
  "currentStatus": 0,
  "receiptPath": "https://storage.blob.core.windows.net/claims/63105a50-e295-4619-8708-c790601c976d/receipt.pdf",
  "createdBy": {
    "id": "323a3afe-711f-4aa6-80d0-f848d24a5340",
    "email": "user3@mail.com",
    "name": "User-3"
```

    },
    "createdOn": 1733450307427,
    "modifiedOn": null
}
```

Look at the terminal logs of the backend background processor as you will see that the message is received and consumed by the action method **api/claimsnotifier/claimsaved** and an information message is logged in the terminal to indicate the processing of the message.

## 5.3.7 Update Backend API to Publish a Message When a Claim Is Saved

We need to update our backend API to publish a message to the message broker when a claim is saved (either due to a new claim being added or an existing claim detail being updated).

To do this, update the **ClaimsStoreManager.cs** under the project **BenefitsManager.Backend.Bff.Api** inside the Services folder as highlighted below.

To avoid duplication, we are not showing the entire file (refer to Chapter 2); however, inside the CreateNewClaimAsync method, before returning claimId, we will add this line:

```
await PublishClaimSavedEvent(claim);
```

Notice the new method **PublishClaimSavedEvent** added to the class. All we have to do is to call the method **PublishClaimSavedEvent** and pass the Pub/Sub name. In our case, we named it **dapr-pubsub-servicebus** as we are going to use Azure Service Bus as a message broker in the next step.

The second parameter, **claimsavedtopic**, represents the topic name to which the publisher will send the task model. These are the only changes needed to begin publishing asynchronous messages from the backend API.
```

```
private async Task PublishClaimSavedEvent(ClaimModel claim)
{
        _logger.LogInformation("Publish claim Saved event
        for claim with Id: '{0}' and Description: '{1}'
        by: '{2}'", claim.ClaimId, claim.Description,
        claim.CreatedBy);
        await _daprClient.PublishEventAsync("dapr-pubsub-
        servicebus", "claimsavedtopic", claim);
}
```

5.4 Use Azure Service Bus As a Service Broker for Dapr Pub/Sub API

Now we will switch our implementation to use Azure Service Bus as a message broker. Redis worked perfectly for local development and testing, but we need to prepare ourselves for the cloud deployment. To do so, we need to create a Service Bus Namespace followed by a Topic. A namespace provides a scoping container for Service Bus resources within your application.

5.4.1 Create an Azure Service Bus Namespace and a Topic

You can do this from the Azure portal or use the PowerShell command below to create the services. We will assume you are using the same PowerShell session from the previous module so variables still hold the right values (otherwise, please refer to Chapters 2 and 3 to get these variable names for $RESOURCE_GROUP, etc.).

You need to change the namespace variable as this one should be unique globally across all Azure subscriptions. Also, you will notice that we are opting for standard SKU (default if not passed) as topics are only

CHAPTER 5   ASYNC COMMUNICATION WITH DAPR PUB/SUB API

available on the standard tier and not on the basic tier. More details about the parameters can be found here: https://learn.microsoft.com/en-us/cli/azure/servicebus/namespace?view=azure-cli-latest#az-servicebus-namespace-create-optional-parameters.

```
$SERVICE_BUS_NAMESPACE_NAME="sbns-claimstracker-$RANDOM_STRING"
$SERVICE_BUS_TOPIC_NAME="claimsavedtopic"
$SERVICE_BUS_TOPIC_SUBSCRIPTION="sbts-claims-processor"
# Create servicebus namespace
az servicebus namespace create --resource-group $RESOURCE_GROUP
--name $SERVICE_BUS_NAMESPACE_NAME --location $LOCATION --sku
Standard

# Create a topic under the namespace
az servicebus topic create --resource-group $RESOURCE_GROUP
--namespace-name $SERVICE_BUS_NAMESPACE_NAME --name $SERVICE_
BUS_TOPIC_NAME

# Create a topic subscription
az servicebus topic subscription create `
--resource-group $RESOURCE_GROUP `
--namespace-name $SERVICE_BUS_NAMESPACE_NAME `
--topic-name $SERVICE_BUS_TOPIC_NAME `
--name $SERVICE_BUS_TOPIC_SUBSCRIPTION

# List connection string
az servicebus namespace authorization-rule keys list `
--resource-group $RESOURCE_GROUP `
--namespace-name $SERVICE_BUS_NAMESPACE_NAME `
--name RootManageSharedAccessKey `
--query primaryConnectionString `
--output tsv
```

CHAPTER 5   ASYNC COMMUNICATION WITH DAPR PUB/SUB API

> **POINT TO NOTE**
>
> Primary connection string is only needed for local dev testing. We can switch to Managed Identities when publishing container apps to Azure Container Apps.

5.4.2 Create a Local Dapr Component File for Pub/Sub API Using Azure Service Bus

We need to add a new Dapr Azure Service Bus Topic component (for more details, refer to https://docs.dapr.io/reference/components-reference/supported-pubsub/setup-azure-servicebus-topics). Add a new file, **"dapr-pubsub-svcbus.yaml"**, in the components folder as shown below. Be sure to update the connection string value.

```
apiVersion: dapr.io/v1alpha1
kind: Component
metadata:
  name: dapr-pubsub-servicebus
spec:
  type: pubsub.azure.servicebus.topics
  version: v1
  metadata:
    - name: connectionString # Used for local dev testing.
      value: "<connection string from step 1 starting with Endpoint=sb://...>"
    - name: consumerID
      value: "sbts-claims-processor"
scopes:
  - Benefitsmanager-Backend-Bff-Api
  - Benefitsmanager-Backend-Processor
```

> **POINT TO NOTE**
>
> We used the name dapr-pubsub-servicebus, which should match the name of the Pub/Sub component we've used earlier in the ClaimsNotifierController.cs controller on the action method with the attribute Topic.
>
> We set the metadata (key/value) to allow us to connect to the Azure Service Bus Topic. The metadata consumerID value should match the topic subscription name sbts-claims-processor.
>
> We have set the scopes section to include the Benefitsmanager-Backend-Bff-Api and Benefitsmanager-Backend-Processor app ids, as those will be the Dapr apps that need access to Azure Service Bus for publishing and consuming the messages.

5.4.3 Create an ACA Dapr Component File for Pub/Sub API Using Azure Service Bus

Add a new file, "**Containerapps-pubsub-svcbus.yaml**", to aca-components as shown below:

```yaml
# pubsub.yaml for Azure Service Bus component
componentType: pubsub.azure.servicebus.topics
version: v1
metadata:
  - name: namespaceName
    value: "sbns-claimstracker-<$RANDOM_STRING>.servicebus.windows.net"
  - name: consumerID
    value: "sbts-claims-processor"
```

CHAPTER 5   ASYNC COMMUNICATION WITH DAPR PUB/SUB API

```
# Application scopes
scopes:
  - Benefitsmanager-Backend-Bff-Api
  - Benefitsmanager-Backend-Processor
```

> **POINT TO NOTE**
>
> We didn't specify the component name **dapr-pubsub-servicebus** when we created this component file. We are going to specify it once we add this Dapr component to the Azure Container Apps environment via CLI.
>
> We are not referencing any service bus connection strings as the authentication between Dapr and Azure Service Bus will be configured using Managed Identities.
>
> The metadata **namespaceName** value is set to the address of the Service Bus namespace as a fully qualified domain name. The namespaceName key is mandatory when using Managed Identities for authentication.
>
> We are setting the metadata **consumerID** value to match the topic subscription name **sbts-claims-processor**. If you didn't set this metadata, Dapr runtime will try to create a subscription using the Dapr application ID.

With all those bits in place, we are ready to re-run the publisher service "Backend API" and the consumer service "Backend Background Service" and test the Pub/Sub pattern end to end.

To run the Backend API project:

```
Cd ~/BenefitsManager.Backend.BFF.API

dapr run `
--app-id BenefitsManager-Backend-Bff-Api `
--app-port $API_APP_PORT `
--dapr-http-port 3500 `
--app-ssl `
```

CHAPTER 5   ASYNC COMMUNICATION WITH DAPR PUB/SUB API

```
--scheduler-host-address "" `
--resources-path "../components" `
-- dotnet run --launch-profile https
```

To run the Backend Background Service project:

```
Cd ~/BenefitsManager.Processor.Backend.Svc
$BACKEND_SERVICE_APP_PORT = <backend service https port in
Properties->launchSettings.json (e.g. 7148)>

dapr run `
--app-id BenefitsManager-Backend-Processor `
--app-port $BACKEND_SERVICE_APP_PORT `
--dapr-http-port 3502 `
--app-ssl `
--scheduler-host-address "" `
--resources-path "../components" `
-- dotnet run --launch-profile https
```

Now let's try to publish a message by sending a POST request to http://localhost:3500/v1.0/publish/**dapr-pubsub-servicebus**/claimsavedtopic with the below request body; don't forget to set the Content-Type header to application/json.

```
POST /v1.0/publish/dapr-pubsub-servicebus/claimsavedtopic
HTTP/1.1
Host: localhost:3500
Content-Type: application/json

    {
      "claimId": "59E029B1-1621-45A1-8263-A77AA7758FAE",
      "merchant": "Merchant-10",
      "claimedAmount": 80,
      "approvedAmount": null,
```

```
    "purchaseDate": 1733201907427,
    "category": {
      "categoryCode": "CAT004",
      "parentCategoryName": "Fitness Activities",
      "categoryName": "Gym"
    },
    "description": "Random description2",
    "statusLog": [
      {
        "status": 0,
        "comment": "",
        "setBy": {
          "id": "323a3afe-711f-4aa6-80d0-f848d24a5340",
          "email": "user3@mail.com",
          "name": "User-3"
        },
        "ts": 1733450307427
      }
    ],
    "currentStatus": 0,
    "receiptPath": "https://storage.blob.core.windows.net/
claims/63105a50-e295-4619-8708-c790601c976d/receipt.pdf",
    "createdBy": {
      "id": "323a3afe-711f-4aa6-80d0-f848d24a5340",
      "email": "user3@mail.com",
      "name": "User-3"
    },
    "createdOn": 1733450307427,
    "modifiedOn": null
}
```

You should see console messages from APP in the backend service console as you send requests.

5.5 Deploy the Backend Background Processor

5.5.1 Build the Backend Background Processor and the Backend API App Images and Push Them to ACR

As we have done previously in Chapters 2 and 3, we need to build and deploy both app images to ACR, so they are ready to be deployed to Azure Container Apps.

Make sure you are in the root directory of the project when running the below commands:

```
$BACKEND_SERVICE_NAME="claimsmanager-backend-processor"

az acr build `
--registry $AZURE_CONTAINER_REGISTRY_NAME `
--image "benefitsmanager/$BE_BFF_API_NAME" `
--file 'BenefitsManager.Backend.Bff.Api/Dockerfile' .

az acr build `
--registry $AZURE_CONTAINER_REGISTRY_NAME `
--image "benefitsmanager/$BACKEND_SERVICE_NAME" `
--file 'BenefitsManager.Processor.Backend.Svc/Dockerfile' .
```

5.5.2 Create a New Azure Container App to Host the New Backend Background Processor

Now we need to create a new Azure container app. We need to have this new container app with those capabilities in place:

- Ingress for this container app should be disabled (no access via HTTP at all as this is a background processor responsible to process published messages).
- Dapr needs to be enabled.

To achieve the above, run the PowerShell script below:

```
az containerapp create `
--name "$BACKEND_SERVICE_NAME" `
--resource-group $RESOURCE_GROUP `
--environment $ENVIRONMENT `
--image "$AZURE_CONTAINER_REGISTRY_NAME.azurecr.io/claimsmanager/$BACKEND_SERVICE_NAME" `
--registry-server "$AZURE_CONTAINER_REGISTRY_NAME.azurecr.io" `
--min-replicas 1 `
--max-replicas 1 `
--cpu 0.25 `
--memory 0.5Gi `
--enable-dapr `
--dapr-app-id $BACKEND_SERVICE_NAME `
--dapr-app-port $TARGET_PORT
```

5.5.3 Deploy New Revisions of the Backend API to Azure Container Apps

We need to update the Azure container app hosting the backend API with a new revision so our code changes for publishing messages after a claim is saved are available for users.

```
# Update Backend API App container app and create a new revision
az containerapp update `
--name $BACKEND_API_NAME `
--resource-group $RESOURCE_GROUP `
--revision-suffix v$TODAY-2
```

5.5.4 Add the Azure Service Bus Dapr Pub/Sub Component to the Azure Container Apps Environment

Deploy the Dapr Pub/Sub component to the Azure Container Apps environment using the below command:

```
az containerapp env dapr-component set `
--name $ENVIRONMENT `
--resource-group $RESOURCE_GROUP `
--dapr-component-name dapr-pubsub-servicebus `
--yaml '.\aca-components\containerapps-pubsub-svcbus.yaml'
```

Notice that we set the component name dapr-pubsub-servicebus when we added it to the container apps environment.

5.6 Summary

In this chapter, we explored how Azure Container Apps uses the Publisher-Subscriber (Pub/Sub) pattern with Dapr and introduced a new background service, ACA Processor – Backend, configured for Dapr. We also introduced Azure Service Bus as a service broker for Dapr Pub/Sub API and tested the Pub/Sub pattern end to end.

We also explored PowerShell scripts to deploy a new background processor app along with updating and revising previously deployed backend APIs to Azure Container Apps.

CHAPTER 6

ACA with Dapr Bindings and Scheduled Jobs with Dapr Cron Binding

In this chapter, we will delve into Dapr bindings as fundamental building blocks and explore how to schedule jobs using Cron bindings. The learning objectives for this chapter include the following:

- Learn how to interface with external systems.
- Extend the backend background processor service (ACA-Processor Backend) to interface with an external system.
- Use Azure Key Vault via a Dapr secret store component to externalize secrets.
- Learn how the Cron binding can trigger actions.
- Add a Cron binding to the backend background processor.
- Deploy updated Background Processor and API projects to Azure.

6.1 Interfacing with an External System

To achieve interfacing with an external system in a simple way, we will utilize **Dapr Input and Output Bindings** (for more details, refer to https://docs.dapr.io/developing-applications/building-blocks/bindings/bindings-overview/).

The external system owns an Azure Storage Queue which the **Benefits Manager** microservice application reacts to through an event handler (**a.k.a. Input Binding**). This event handler receives and processes the message coming to the storage queue. Once the processing of the message completes and stores the task into Cosmos DB, the system will trigger an event (**a.k.a. Output Binding**) that invokes the external service. This service, in turn, stores the content of the message into an Azure Blob Storage container. It is important to emphasize that both the Azure Storage Queue and the Azure Storage Blob belong to the external system.

The rest of this chapter will implement the two scenarios mentioned below:

- Trigger a process on the ACA-Processor Backend based on a message sent to a specific Azure Storage Queue. This scenario will assume that the Azure Storage Queue is an external system to which external clients can submit tasks.

- From the service ACA-Processor Backend, we will invoke an external resource that stores the content of the incoming task from the external queue as a JSON blob file on Azure Storage Blobs.

Figure 6-1 provides a high-level architecture to understand the flow of input and output bindings in Dapr.

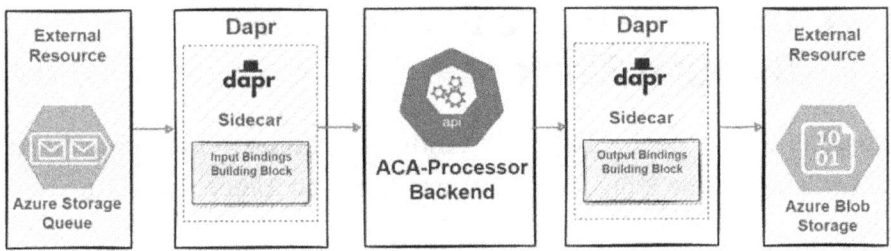

Figure 6-1. *Dapr Input and Output bindings building block*

If you look at Dapr Bindings building block, you will notice a lot of similarities with the Pub/Sub building block that we covered in Chapter 5. But remember that the Pub/Sub building block is meant to be used for async communication between services within your solution. The Binding building block has a wider scope, and it mainly focuses on connectivity and interoperability across different systems, disparate applications, and services outside the boundaries of your own application. For a full list of supported bindings, refer to this link `https://docs.dapr.io/reference/components-reference/supported-bindings/`.

> **POINT TO NOTE**
>
> Those third-party external services could be services hosted on another cloud provider, different Azure subscription, or even on premises. Dapr bindings are usually used to trigger an application with events coming in from external systems as well as interface with external systems.
>
> To make it simple, we are going to host those two supposedly external services in the same subscription of our Benefits Manager microservice application.

CHAPTER 6   ACA WITH DAPR BINDINGS AND SCHEDULED JOBS WITH DAPR CRON BINDING

6.1.1 Overview of the Dapr Bindings Building Block

Figure 6-2 shows the detailed Dapr bindings building block architecture diagram that we are going to implement in this chapter to fulfill the use case we discussed in the beginning of this section.

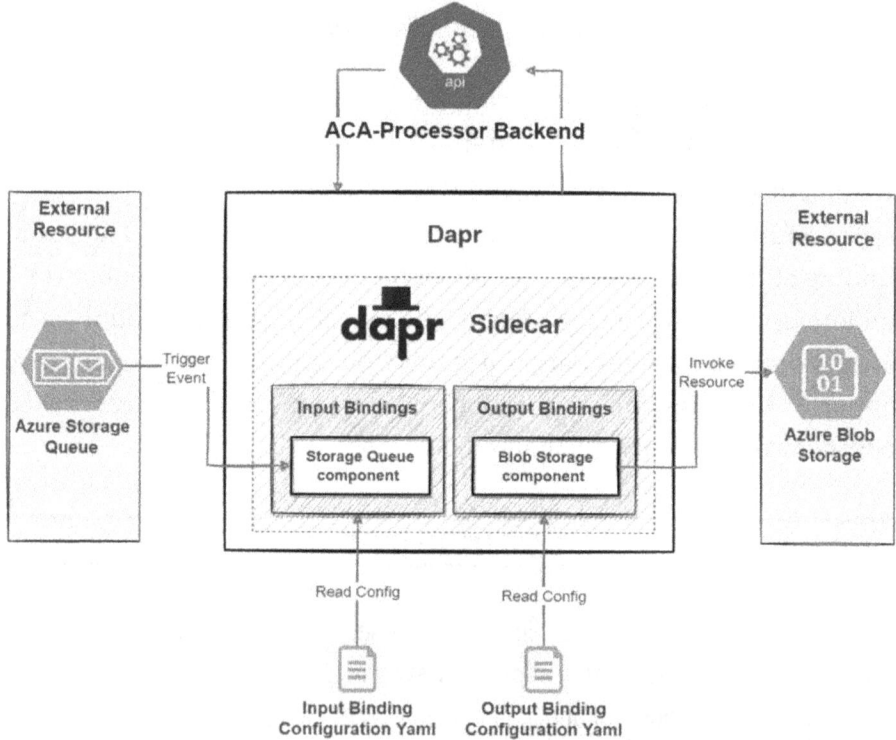

Figure 6-2. *Detailed architecture of the Dapr building blocks*

Looking at the diagram, we notice the following:

- In order to receive events and data from the external resource (Azure Storage Queue), our **ACA-Processor Backend service** needs to register a public endpoint that will become an event handler.

178

- This binding configuration between the external resource and our service will be configured by using the **Input Binding Configuration YAML file**. The Dapr sidecar of the background service will read the configuration and subscribe to the endpoint defined for the external resource. In our case, it will be a specific Azure Storage Queue.

- When a message is published to the storage queue, the input binding component running in the Dapr sidecar picks it up and triggers the event.

- The Dapr sidecar invokes the endpoint (event handler defined in the ACA-Processor Backend service) configured for the binding. In our case, it will be an endpoint that can be reached by invoking a POST operation **http://localhost:3502/ExternalTasksProcessor/Process**, and the request body content will be the JSON payload of the published message to the Azure Storage Queue.

- When the event is handled in our **ACA-Processor Backend** and the business logic is completed, this endpoint needs to return an HTTP response with a **200 OK** status to acknowledge that processing is complete. If the event handling is not completed or there is an error, this endpoint should return an HTTP **4xx or 5xx** status code.

- In order to enable the service **ACA-Processor Backend** to trigger an event that invokes an external resource, we need to use the **Output Binding Configuration YAML file** to configure the binding between our service and the external resource (Azure Blob Storage) and how to connect to it.

CHAPTER 6   ACA WITH DAPR BINDINGS AND SCHEDULED JOBS WITH DAPR CRON BINDING

- Once the Dapr sidecar reads the binding configuration file, our service can trigger an event that invokes the output binding API on the Dapr sidecar. In our case, the event will be creating a new blob file containing the content of the message we read earlier from the Azure Storage Queue.

- With this in place, our service **ACA-Processor Backend** will be ready to invoke the external resource by sending a POST operation to the endpoint `http://localhost:3502/v1.0/bindings/ExternalTasksBlobstore`, and the JSON payload will contain the content below. Alternatively, we can use the Dapr client SDK to invoke this output binding to invoke the external service and store the file in Azure Blob Storage.

```
{
    "data": {
      "claimId": "59E029B1-1621-45A1-8263-A77AA7758FAE",
      "merchant": "Merchant-10",
      "claimedAmount": 80,
      "approvedAmount": null,
      "purchaseDate": 1733201907427,
      "category": {
        "categoryCode": "CAT004",
        "parentCategoryName": "Fitness Activities",
        "categoryName": "Gym"
      },
      "description": "Random description2",
      "statusLog": [
```

```json
{
    "status": 0,
    "comment": "",
    "setBy": {
      "id": "323a3afe-711f-4aa6-80d0-
      f848d24a5340",
      "email": "user3@mail.com",
      "name": "User-3"
    },
    "ts": 1733450307427
  }
],
"currentStatus": 0,
"receiptPath": "https://storage.blob.core.
windows.net/claims/63105a50-e295-4619-8708-
c790601c976d/receipt.pdf",
"createdBy": {
  "id": "323a3afe-711f-4aa6-80d0-f848d24a5340",
  "email": "user3@mail.com",
  "name": "User-3"
},
"createdOn": 1733450307427,
"modifiedOn": null
  },
  "operation": "create"
}
```

Let's start by updating our backend background processor project and define the input and output bindings configuration files and event handlers.

CHAPTER 6   ACA WITH DAPR BINDINGS AND SCHEDULED JOBS WITH DAPR CRON BINDING

We need to provision the Azure Storage Account to start responding to messages published to a queue and then later use the same storage account to store blob files as an external event. Run the PowerShell script below to create the Azure Storage Account and get the master key.

```
$STORAGE_ACCOUNT_NAME = "stbenefitstracker$RANDOM_STRING"

az storage account create `
--name $STORAGE_ACCOUNT_NAME `
--resource-group $RESOURCE_GROUP `
--location $LOCATION `
--sku Standard_LRS `
--kind StorageV2

# List Azure storage keys
az storage account keys list `
--resource-group $RESOURCE_GROUP `
--account-name $STORAGE_ACCOUNT_NAME

# Get the primary storage account key
$STORAGE_ACCOUNT_KEY=($(az storage account keys list `
--resource-group $RESOURCE_GROUP `
--account-name $STORAGE_ACCOUNT_NAME `
--output json) | ConvertFrom-Json)[0].value

echo "Storage Account Name : $STORAGE_ACCOUNT_NAME"
echo "Storage Account Key  : $STORAGE_ACCOUNT_KEY"
```

Take note of the Storage Account Name and Storage Account Key values as we will use them in later sections.

CHAPTER 6   ACA WITH DAPR BINDINGS AND SCHEDULED JOBS WITH DAPR CRON BINDING

6.2 Updating the Backend Background Processor Project

6.2.1 Create an Event Handler (API Endpoint) to Respond to Messages Published to Azure Storage Queue

We will now add an endpoint that will be responsible to handle the event when a message is published to Azure Storage Queue. This endpoint will start receiving the message published from the external service.

Create a new controller, **ExternalClaimsProcessorController**, inside the controllers folder under the **BenefitsManager.Processor. Backend.Svc**.

```
using Dapr.Client;
using Microsoft.AspNetCore.Mvc;
using BenefitsManager.Common.Models;

namespace BenefitsManager.Processor.Backend.Svc.Controllers
{
    public class ExternalClaimsProcessorController :
    ControllerBase
    {
        private readonly ILogger<ExternalClaimsProcessor
        Controller> _logger;
        private readonly DaprClient _daprClient;

        public ExternalClaimsProcessorController(ILogger
        <ExternalClaimsProcessorController> logger, DaprClient
        daprClient)
        {
            _logger = logger;
```

CHAPTER 6 ACA WITH DAPR BINDINGS AND SCHEDULED JOBS WITH DAPR CRON BINDING

```csharp
        _daprClient = daprClient;
    }

    [HttpPost("process")]
    public async Task<IActionResult> ProcessClaimAndStore
    ([FromBody] ClaimModel claimModel)
    {
        try
        {
            _logger.LogInformation("Started processing
            external task message from storage queue. claim
            Name: '{0}'", claimModel.Description);

            claimModel.ClaimId = Guid.NewGuid();
            claimModel.CreatedOn = DateTime.UtcNow.Ticks;

            //Dapr SideCar Invocation (save claim to a
            state store)
            await _daprClient.InvokeMethodAsync(HttpMethod.
            Post, "benefitsmanager-backend-bff-api", $"api/
            claims", claimModel);

            _logger.LogInformation("Saved external
            claim to the state store successfully.
            claim description: '{0}', Claim Id: '{1}'",
            claimModel.Description, claimModel.ClaimId);

            //TODO: code to invoke external binding and
            store queue message content into blob file in
            Azure storage

            return Ok();
        }
        catch (Exception)
```

```
            {
                throw;
            }
        }
    }
}
```

In the above code, we created a new method named **ProcessClaimAndStore**, which can be accessed by sending HTTP POST operation on the endpoint ExternalTasksProcessor/Process.

This action method accepts the ClaimModel in the request body as JSON payload. This is what will be received from the external service (Azure Storage Queue). Within this action method, we are going to store the received claim by sending a POST request to /api/claims, which is part of the backend API named **benefitsmanager-backend-bff-api**. We return **200 OK** to acknowledge that the message received is processed successfully and should be removed from the external service queue.

6.2.2 Create the Dapr Input Binding Component File

Let's create the component configuration file that will describe the configuration as well as how our backend background processor will start handling events coming from the external service (Azure Storage Queues). Add a new file, "**dapr-bindings-in-storagequeue.yaml**", under the components folder.

```
apiVersion: dapr.io/v1alpha1
kind: Component
metadata:
  name: externalclaimsmanager
```

```
spec:
  type: bindings.azure.storagequeues
  version: v1
  metadata:
  - name: storageAccount
    value: "<Your Storage Account Name>"
  - name: storageAccessKey
    value: "<Your Storage Account Key>"
  - name: queue
    value: "external-claims-queue"
  - name: decodeBase64
    value: "true"
  - name: route
    value: /externalclaimsprocessor/process
```

> **POINT TO NOTE**
>
> Make sure to replace **<Your Storage Account Name>** and **<Your Storage Account Key>** in the above YAML file with the values from Section 6.1.1.

For full specifications of the YAML file with **Azure Storage Queues**, refer to https://docs.dapr.io/reference/components-reference/supported-bindings/storagequeues/; however, let's go over the configuration we have added here:

- The type of binding is **bindings.azure.storagequeues**.
- The name of this input binding is **externalclaimsmanager**.

- We are setting the **storageAccount** name, **storageAccessKey** value, and the **queue** name. Those properties will describe how the event handler we added can connect to the external service. You can create any queue you prefer on the Azure Storage Account we created to simulate an external system.

- We are setting the route property to the value / **externalclaimsprocessor/process**, which is the address of the endpoint we have just added, so POST requests are sent to this endpoint.

- We are setting the property **decodeBase64** to true as the messages queued in the Azure Storage Queue are Base64 encoded.

6.2.3 Create the Dapr Output Binding Component File

Let's create the component configuration file that will describe the configuration and how our **ACA-Processor Backend** will be able to invoke the external service (Azure Blob Storage) and be able to create and store a JSON blob file that contains the content of the message received from Azure Storage Queues. Add a new file, "**dapr-bindings-out-storagequeue.yaml**", under the components folder.

```
apiVersion: dapr.io/v1alpha1
kind: Component
metadata:
  name: externalclaimsblobstore
spec:
  type: bindings.azure.blobstorage
  version: v1
```

```
metadata:
  - name: storageAccount
    value: "<Your Storage Account Name>"
  - name: storageAccessKey
    value: "<Your Storage Account Key>"
  - name: container
    value: "externalclaimscontainer"
  - name: decodeBase64
    value: false
```

> **POINT TO NOTE**
>
> Make sure to replace **<Your Storage Account Name>** and **<Your Storage Account Key>** in the above YAML file with the values from Section 6.1.1.

For full specifications of the YAML file with **Azure Storage Queues**, refer to `https://docs.dapr.io/reference/components-reference/supported-bindings/blobstorage/`; however, let's go over the configuration we have added here:

- The type of binding is **bindings.azure.blobstorage**.

- The name of this output binding is **externalclaimsblobstore**. We will use this name when we use the Dapr SDK to trigger the output binding.

- We are setting the **storageAccount** name, **storageAccessKey** value, and the **container** name. Those properties will describe how our backend background service will be able to connect to the external service and create a blob file. We will assume that there is a container already created on the external service and named **externalclaimscontainer** as shown in the image below.

- We set the **decodeBase64** property to false because we do not want to encode the file content as Base64 images; instead, we need to store the file content in its original form.

6.2.4 Use Dapr Client SDK to Invoke the Output Binding

Let's invoke the output binding by using the .NET SDK. Update and replace the code in the **ExternalClaimsProcessorController.cs** as shown below:

```
using Dapr.Client;
using Microsoft.AspNetCore.Mvc;
using BenefitsManager.Common.Models;

namespace BenefitsManager.Processor.Backend.Svc.Controllers
{
    public class ExternalClaimsProcessorController : ControllerBase
    {
        private readonly ILogger<ExternalClaimsProcessorController> _logger;
        private readonly DaprClient _daprClient;

        private const string OUTPUT_BINDING_NAME = "externalclaimsblobstore";
        private const string OUTPUT_BINDING_OPERATION = "create";

        public ExternalClaimsProcessorController(ILogger
        <ExternalClaimsProcessorController> logger, DaprClient daprClient)
```

CHAPTER 6 ACA WITH DAPR BINDINGS AND SCHEDULED JOBS WITH DAPR CRON BINDING

```
{
    _logger = logger;
    _daprClient = daprClient;
}

[HttpPost("process")]
public async Task<IActionResult>
ProcessClaimAndStore([FromBody] ClaimModel claimModel)
{
    try
    {
        _logger.LogInformation("Started processing
        external task message from storage queue. claim
        Name: '{0}'", claimModel.Description);

        claimModel.ClaimId = Guid.NewGuid();
        claimModel.CreatedOn = DateTime.UtcNow.Ticks;

        //Dapr SideCar Invocation (save claim to a
        state store)
        await _daprClient.InvokeMethodAsync(HttpMethod.
        Post, "benefitsmanager-backend-api", $"api/
        claims", claimModel);

        _logger.LogInformation("Saved external
        claim to the state store successfully.
        Claim description: '{0}', Claim Id: '{1}'",
        claimModel.Description, claimModel.ClaimId);

        //code to invoke external binding and store
        queue message content into blob file in
        Azure storage
        IReadOnlyDictionary<string, string> metaData =
        new Dictionary<string, string>()
```

```csharp
            {
                { "blobName", $"{claimModel.ClaimId}.
                json" },
            };

            await _daprClient.InvokeBindingAsync
            (OUTPUT_BINDING_NAME, OUTPUT_BINDING_OPERATION,
            claimModel, metaData);

            _logger.LogInformation("Invoked output binding
            '{0}' for external task. Claim description:
            '{1}', Claim Id: '{2}'", OUTPUT_BINDING_NAME,
            claimModel.Description, claimModel.ClaimId);

            return Ok();
        }
        catch (Exception)
        {
            throw;
        }
    }
}
```

Looking at the **ProcessClaimAndStore** action method above, you will see that we are calling the method **InvokeBindingAsync** and we are passing the binding name **externalclaimsblobstore** defined in the configuration file, as well as the second parameter **create**, which is the action we need to carry against the external blob storage.

You can also delete or retrieve the content of a specific file. For a complete list of supported actions on Azure Blob Storage, refer to https://docs.dapr.io/reference/components-reference/supported-bindings/blobstorage/#binding-support.

CHAPTER 6   ACA WITH DAPR BINDINGS AND SCHEDULED JOBS WITH DAPR CRON BINDING

Notice that we are setting the file name and storing it on the external service. We need the file names to be created using the same claim identifier, so we will pass the key **blobName** with the file name values into the **metaData** dictionary.

6.2.5 Test Dapr Bindings Locally

To try this out, we are now ready to do an end-to-end test on our dev machine. To accomplish this, run the following commands in three separate PowerShell windows, ensuring that you are in the correct root folder for each respective project.

To run the Backend API project:

```
Cd ~/BenefitsManager.Backend.BFF.API

dapr run `
--app-id BenefitsManager-Backend-Bff-Api `
--app-port $API_APP_PORT `
--dapr-http-port 3500 `
--app-ssl `
--scheduler-host-address "" `
--resources-path "../components" `
-- dotnet run --launch-profile https
```

To run the Backend Background Service project:

```
Cd ~/BenefitsManager.Processor.Backend.Svc

$BACKEND_SERVICE_APP_PORT = <backend service https port in Properties->launchSettings.json (e.g. 7148)>

dapr run `
--app-id BenefitsManager-Backend-Processor `
--app-port $BACKEND_SERVICE_APP_PORT `
--dapr-http-port 3502 `
```

CHAPTER 6   ACA WITH DAPR BINDINGS AND SCHEDULED JOBS WITH DAPR CRON BINDING

```
--app-ssl `
--scheduler-host-address "" `
--resources-path "../components" `
-- dotnet run --launch-profile https
```

To run the Frontend UI project:

```
Cd  ~/BenefitsManager.Frontend.WebPortal.Ui

dapr run `
--app-id BenefitsManager-Frontend-WebPortal-Ui `
--app-port $UI_APP_PORT `
--dapr-http-port 3501 `
--app-ssl `
--resources-path "../components" `
-- dotnet run --launch-profile https
```

Open Azure Storage Explorer on your local machine. If you don't have it installed, you can install it by downloading it from this link: https://azure.microsoft.com/en-us/products/storage/storage-explorer/#overview. Log in to your Azure subscription and navigate to the storage account already created, create a queue, and use the same name you already used in the Dapr Input configuration file. In our case, the name of the queue in the configuration file is **external-claims-queue**.

The content of the message that Azure Storage Queue accepts should be as below, so try to queue a new message using the tool as shown below:

```
{
    "claimId": "59E029B1-1621-45A1-8263-A77AA7758FAE",
    "merchant": "Merchant-10",
    "claimedAmount": 80,
    "approvedAmount": null,
    "purchaseDate": 1733201907427,
    "category": {
```

CHAPTER 6   ACA WITH DAPR BINDINGS AND SCHEDULED JOBS WITH DAPR CRON BINDING

```
      "categoryCode": "CAT004",
      "parentCategoryName": "Fitness Activities",
      "categoryName": "Gym"
    },
    "description": "Random description2",
    "statusLog": [
      {
        "status": 0,
        "comment": "",
        "setBy": {
          "id": "323a3afe-711f-4aa6-80d0-f848d24a5340",
          "email": "user3@mail.com",
          "name": "User-3"
        },
        "ts": 1733450307427
      }
    ],
    "currentStatus": 0,
    "receiptPath": "https://storage.blob.core.windows.net/
    claims/63105a50-e295-4619-8708-c790601c976d/receipt.pdf",
    "createdBy": {
      "id": "323a3afe-711f-4aa6-80d0-f848d24a5340",
      "email": "user3@mail.com",
      "name": "User-3"
    },
    "createdOn": 1733450307427,
    "modifiedOn": null
}
```

If everything has been successfully configured as described in the previous sections, you should see a JSON file created as a blob in the Azure Storage container named "**externalclaimscontainer**", based on our configuration.

6.3 Configure a Dapr Secret Store Component with Azure Key Vault

We have three Dapr components that are not Microsoft Entra ID enabled. Since these component files are storing sensitive keys to access different external services, the recommended approach for retrieving these secrets is to reference an existing Dapr secret store component that can securely access these secrets.

We need to create a **Dapr secret store component** using the container apps schema (for more details, refer to https://docs.dapr.io/developing-applications/building-blocks/secrets/secrets-overview/). The Dapr secret store will be configured with the Azure Key Vault secret store (for more details, refer to https://docs.dapr.io/reference/components-reference/supported-secret-stores/azure-keyvault/).

6.3.1 Create an Azure Key Vault Resource

Create an Azure Key Vault that will be used to store securely any secret or key used in our application. Open the Azure CLI window to run the below command:

```
$KEYVAULT_NAME = "kv-claims-tracker-$RANDOM_STRING"

az keyvault create `
--name $KEYVAULT_NAME `
--resource-group $RESOURCE_GROUP `
--location $LOCATION `
--enable-rbac-authorization true
```

> **POINT TO NOTE**
>
> It is essential to create the Azure Key Vault with Azure RBAC for authorization by setting **--enable-rbac-authorization** to true, as the role assigned to the Microsoft Entra ID application will function only when RBAC authorization is enabled.

6.3.2 Grant Backend Processor App a Role to Read Secrets from Azure Key Vault

In Chapter 5, we have configured the system-assigned identity for the service ACA-Processor Backend. In this section, we will assign a role named **Key Vault Secrets User** to it, so it can access and read secrets from the above created Azure Key Vault. Execute the below code from the Azure CLI window to do role assignment.

```
$KEYVAULT_SECRETS_USER_ROLE_ID = "4633458b-17de-408a-b874-0445c86b69e6" # ID for 'Key Vault Secrets User' Role

# Get PRINCIPAL ID of BACKEND Processor Service
$BACKEND_SERVICE_PRINCIPAL_ID = az containerapp show `
--name $BACKEND_SERVICE_NAME `
--resource-group $RESOURCE_GROUP `
--query identity.principalId `
--output tsv

az role assignment create `
--role $KEYVAULT_SECRETS_USER_ROLE_ID `
--assignee $BACKEND_SERVICE_PRINCIPAL_ID `
--scope "/subscriptions/$AZURE_SUBSCRIPTION_ID/resourcegroups/$RESOURCE_GROUP/providers/Microsoft.KeyVault/vaults/$KEYVAULT_NAME"
```

CHAPTER 6   ACA WITH DAPR BINDINGS AND SCHEDULED JOBS WITH DAPR CRON BINDING

For more details about Azure built-in role for Key Vault data plane operations, refer to https://learn.microsoft.com/en-us/azure/key-vault/general/rbac-guide?tabs=azure-cli#azure-built-in-roles-for-key-vault-data-plane-operations.

6.3.3 Create Secrets in the Azure Key Vault

Using the Azure CLI, we will assign the Key Vault Secrets Officer role to the signed-in user to enable secret creation. Execute the following commands to accomplish this:

```
$SIGNEDIN_USERID = az ad signed-in-user show --query id --output tsv
$KEYVAULT_SECRETS_OFFICER_ROLE_ID = "b86a8fe4-44ce-4948-aee5-eccb2c155cd7" # ID for 'Key Vault Secrets Office' Role

az role assignment create `
--role $KEYVAULT_SECRETS_OFFICER_ROLE_ID `
--assignee $SIGNEDIN_USERID `
--scope "/subscriptions/$AZURE_SUBSCRIPTION_ID/resourcegroups/$RESOURCE_GROUP/providers/Microsoft.KeyVault/vaults/$KEYVAULT_NAME"
```

We will create the secrets in the Azure Key Vault using the commands below:

```
# Set External Azure Storage Access Key as a secret named 'external-azure-storage-key'
az keyvault secret set `
--vault-name $KEYVAULT_NAME `
--name "external-azure-storage-key" `
--value $STORAGE_ACCOUNT_KEY
```

6.3.4 Create an ACA Dapr Secrets Store Component File

Create a new YAML file named "containerapps-secretstore-kv.yaml" inside the aca-components folder, as shown below:

```yaml
componentType: secretstores.azure.keyvault
version: v1
metadata:
  - name: vaultName
    value: <Your keyvault name from $KEYVAULT_NAME goes here>
scopes:
  - Benefitsmanager-Backend-Processor
```

- We didn't specify the component name **secretstoreakv** in the metadata of this component YAML file. We are going to specify it once we add this Dapr component to the Azure Container Apps environment via CLI similar to what we did in other chapters.

- We are not referencing any service bus connection strings as the authentication between Dapr and Azure Service Bus will be configured using Managed Identities.

- The metadata **vaultName** value is set to the name of the Azure Key Vault we've just created.

- We are allowing this component only to be accessed by the Dapr with application ID **Benefitsmanager-Backend-Processor**. This means that our backend API or frontend web app services will not be able to access the Dapr secret store. If we want to allow them to access the secrets, we need to update this component file and grant the system-identity of those services a **Key Vault Secrets User** role.

6.3.5 Create Input and Output Binding Component Files Matching Azure Container Apps Specs

Create two new files named "**containerapps-bindings-in-storagequeue.yaml**" and "**containerapps-bindings-out-blobstorage.yaml**" under the aca-components folder as shown below.

containerapps-bindings-in-storagequeue.yaml

```
componentType: bindings.azure.storagequeues
version: v1
secretStoreComponent: "secretstoreakv"
metadata:
  - name: storageAccount
    value: "<Your Storage Account Name>"
  - name: storageAccessKey
    secretRef: external-azure-storage-key
  - name: queue
    value: "external-tasks-queue"
  - name: decodeBase64
    value: "true"
  - name: route
    value: /externalclaimsprocessor/process
scopes:
  - Benefitsmanager-Backend-Processor
```

The properties of this file are matching the ones used in the Dapr component-specific file. It is a component of type **bindings.azure.storagequeues**. The only differences are the following:

- We are setting the property secretStoreComponent value to **secretstoreakv**, which is the name of the Dapr secret store component.

- We are using **secretRef** when setting the metadata **storageAccessKey**. The value **external-azure-storage-key** represents the AKV secret created earlier.

containerapps-bindings-out-blobstorage.yaml

```
componentType: bindings.azure.blobstorage
version: v1
secretStoreComponent: "secretstoreakv"
metadata:
  - name: storageAccount
    value: "<Your Storage Account Name>"
  - name: storageAccessKey
    secretRef: external-azure-storage-key
  - name: container
    value: "externalclaimscontainer"
  - name: decodeBase64
    value: "false"
  - name: publicAccessLevel
    value: "none"
scopes:
  - Benefitsmanager-Backend-Processor
```

The properties of this file are matching the ones used in the Dapr component-specific file. It is a component of type **bindings.azure.blobstorage**. The only differences are the following:

- We are setting the property **secretStoreComponent** value to **secretstoreakv**, which is the name of the **Dapr secret store** component.

- We are using **secretRef** when setting the metadata **storageAccessKey**. The value **external-azure-storage-key** represents the AKV secret created earlier.

Ensure that you replace **<Your Storage Account Name>** with the correct values. With those changes in place, we are ready to rebuild the backend background processor container image, update the Azure Container Apps environment, and redeploy a new revision.

6.4 Cron Bindings

There is a special type of Dapr Input binding named **Cron binding**. The Cron binding doesn't subscribe to events coming from an external system. Instead, this binding can be used to trigger application code in our service periodically based on a configurable interval. The binding provides a simple way to implement a background worker to wake up and do some work at a regular interval, without the need to implement an endless loop with a configurable delay. We intend to utilize this binding for a specific use case, wherein it will be triggered once daily at a particular time (12:05 a.m.), and search for all claims that have a due date matching the previous day of its execution and are still pending. Once the service identifies claims that meet these criteria, it will designate them as overdue claims and save the revised status on Azure Cosmos DB. In contrast to Azure Container Apps Jobs, Cron bindings do not need a separate container app and can integrate this binding into our existing backend service.

6.4.1 Add a Cron Binding Configuration

To set up the Cron binding, we add a new component file, "dapr-scheduled-cron.yaml", within the components folder, which specifies the code that requires triggering and the intervals at which it should occur.

CHAPTER 6   ACA WITH DAPR BINDINGS AND SCHEDULED JOBS WITH DAPR CRON BINDING

```
apiVersion: dapr.io/v1alpha1
kind: Component
metadata:
  name: ScheduledClaimsManager
  namespace: default
spec:
  type: bindings.cron
  version: v1
  metadata:
    - name: schedule
      value: "5 0 * * *" # Everyday at 12:05am
scopes:
  - Benefitsmanager-Backend-Processor
```

The above YAML file performs the following actions:

- Adds a new input binding of type **bindings.cron**.

- Provides the name **ScheduledClaimsManager** for this binding. This means that an HTTP POST endpoint on the URL /ScheduledTasksManager should be added as it will be invoked when the job is triggered based on the Cron interval.

- Setting the interval for this Cron job to be triggered once a day at **12:05 a.m**. For full details and available options on how to set this value, visit the Cron binding specs at this link: https://docs.dapr.io/reference/components-reference/supported-bindings/cron/#schedule-format.

CHAPTER 6   ACA WITH DAPR BINDINGS AND SCHEDULED JOBS WITH DAPR CRON BINDING

6.4.2 Add the Endpoint to Be Invoked by Cron Binding

Create a new controller called "**ScheduledClaimsManagerController**" inside the BenefitsManager.Processor.Backend.Svc project under the controllers folder. This acts as an endpoint that will be triggered when the Cron configuration is met. This endpoint will contain the logic needed to run at a regular interval.

```
using Dapr.Client;
using Microsoft.AspNetCore.Mvc;
using BenefitsManager.Common.Models;

namespace BenefitsManager.Processor.Backend.Svc.Controllers
{
    [Route("ScheduledClaimsManager")]
    [ApiController]
    public class ScheduledClaimsManagerController :
    ControllerBase
    {
        private readonly ILogger<ScheduledClaimsManager
        Controller> _logger;
        private readonly DaprClient _daprClient;
        public ScheduledClaimsManagerController(ILogger
        <ScheduledClaimsManagerController> logger, DaprClient
        daprClient)
        {
            _logger = logger;
            _daprClient = daprClient;
        }
```

```csharp
[HttpPost]
public async Task CheckOverDueClaimsJob()
{
    var runAt = DateTime.UtcNow;

    _logger.LogInformation($"ScheduledClaimsManager::
    Timer Services triggered at: {runAt}");

    var overdueClaimsList = new List<ClaimModel>();

    var claimsList = await _daprClient.InvokeMethod
    Async<List<ClaimModel>>(HttpMethod.
    Get, "benefitsmanager-backend-api", $"api/
    overdueclaims");

    _logger.LogInformation($"ScheduledClaimsManager::
    completed query state store for claims, retrieved
    claims count: {claimsList?.Count()}");

    claimsList?.ForEach(claimModel =>
    {
        var purchaseDate = DateTimeOffset.FromUnixTime
        Milliseconds(claimModel.PurchaseDate).
        UtcDateTime;
        if (runAt.Date > purchaseDate.Date)
        {
            overdueClaimsList.Add(claimModel);
        }
    });
```

```
            if (overdueClaimsList.Count > 0)
            {
                _logger.LogInformation($"ScheduledClaimsMana
                ger::marking {overdueClaimsList.Count()} as
                overdue claims");

                await _daprClient.InvokeMethodAsync(HttpMethod.
                Post, "benefitsmanager-backend-api", $"api/
                overdueclaims/markoverdue", overdueClaimsList);
            }
        }
    }
}
```

In the code above, we have introduced a new action method named **"CheckOverDueClaimsJob"**, which encapsulates the business logic to be executed by the Cron job at predefined intervals. This method must be of the **POST** type to ensure it is triggered whenever the job runs according to the specified Cron schedule.

6.4.3 Update the Backend Web API Project

We need to add two new methods that are used by the scheduled job. Open the interface file IClaimsManager.cs, which is in the project "BenefitsManager.Common.Models", and add the two new methods as shown below:

```
namespace BenefitsManager.Common.Models
{
    public interface IClaimsManager
    {
        Task<List<ClaimModel>> GetClaimsByCreatorAsync(string
        userId);
```

CHAPTER 6 ACA WITH DAPR BINDINGS AND SCHEDULED JOBS WITH DAPR CRON BINDING

```
        Task<ClaimModel?> GetClaimByIdAsync(Guid claimId);
        Task<Guid> CreateNewClaimAsync(string merchant, decimal
        claimedAmount, long purchaseDate, string categoryCode,
        string description, string receiptPath, UserModel
        createdBy);
        Task<bool> UpdateClaimAsync(Guid claimId, string
        merchant, decimal claimedAmount, long purchaseDate,
        string categoryCode, string description, string
        receiptPath);
        Task<bool> UpdateClaimStatusAsync(Guid claimId, decimal
        approvedAmount, ClaimStatus newStatus, string comment,
        UserModel setBy);
        Task<bool> DeleteClaimAsync(Guid claimId);
        Task MarkOverdueClaims(List<ClaimModel>
        overdueClaimsList);
        Task<List<ClaimModel>> GetYesterdaysDueClaims();
    }
}
```

Open the class ClaimsStoreManager.cs, which is in the project "BenefitsManager.Backend.Bff.Api", to add implementation details for these two methods. Below code snippets are only for newly added methods to avoid duplication.

```
public async Task MarkOverdueClaims(List<ClaimModel>
overdueClaimsList)
    {
        foreach (var ClaimModel in overdueClaimsList)
        {
            _logger.LogInformation("Mark Claim with Id: '{0}' as
            OverDue task", ClaimModel.ClaimId);
            ClaimModel.IsOverDue = true;
```

```csharp
        await _daprClient.SaveStateAsync(STORE_NAME,
        ClaimModel.ClaimId.ToString(), ClaimModel);
    }
}
public async Task<List<ClaimModel>> GetYesterdaysDueClaims()
{
    var options = new JsonSerializerOptions
    {
        PropertyNamingPolicy = JsonNamingPolicy.CamelCase,
        WriteIndented = true,
        Converters =
        {
            new JsonStringEnumConverter(),
            new DateTimeConverter("yyyy-MM-ddTHH:mm:ss")
        },
        PropertyNameCaseInsensitive = true,
        DefaultIgnoreCondition = JsonIgnoreCondition.
        WhenWritingNull,
        Encoder = JavaScriptEncoder.UnsafeRelaxedJsonEscaping
    };
    var yesterday = DateTime.Today.AddDays(-1);

    var jsonDate = JsonSerializer.Serialize(yesterday,
    options);

    _logger.LogInformation("Getting overdue claims for
    yesterday date: '{0}'", jsonDate);

    var query = "{" +
            "\"filter\": {" +
                "\"EQ\": { \"claimDueDate\": " + jsonDate
                + " }" +
            "}}";
```

CHAPTER 6   ACA WITH DAPR BINDINGS AND SCHEDULED JOBS WITH DAPR CRON BINDING

```
    var queryResponse = await _daprClient.QueryStateAsync<Claim
    Model>(STORE_NAME, query);

    var tasksList = queryResponse.Results
                    .Where(q => q.Data != null)
                    // filter null data
                    .Select(q => q.Data)
                    .Where(q => q!.IsCompleted == false &&
                    q.IsOverDue == false)
                    .OrderBy(o => o!.CreatedOn);

    return tasksList.ToList()!;
}
```

The **GetYesterdaysDueClaims** method will query the Cosmos DB state store using Dapr State API to retrieve all claims from yesterday that have not been completed. Note that Cron jobs are scheduled to run daily at 12:05 a.m., so we are only interested in checking the claims from the day prior to the service execution.

The MarkOverdueClaims method will take a list of all claims that passed the due date and set the flag IsOverDue to true.

Add a new file, "**DateTimeConverter**", inside the Utilities folder in the project "**BenefitsManager.Backend.Bff.Api**" as shown below:

```
using System.Text.Json.Serialization;
using System.Text.Json;

namespace BenefitsManager.Backend.Bff.Api.Utilities
{
    public class DateTimeConverter : JsonConverter<DateTime>
    {
        private readonly string _dateFormatString;

        public DateTimeConverter(string dateFormatString)
```

```
        {
            _dateFormatString = dateFormatString;
        }

        public override DateTime Read(ref Utf8JsonReader
        reader, Type typeToConvert, JsonSerializerOptions
        options)
        {
            var dateString = reader.GetString();

            if (dateString != null)
            {
                return DateTime.ParseExact(dateString, _
                dateFormatString, System.Globalization.
                CultureInfo.InvariantCulture);
            }
            else
            {
                throw new("Date string from reader is null.");
            }
        }

        public override void Write(Utf8JsonWriter writer,
        DateTime value, JsonSerializerOptions options)
        {
            writer.WriteStringValue(value.ToString
            (_dateFormatString));
        }
    }
}
```

CHAPTER 6   ACA WITH DAPR BINDINGS AND SCHEDULED JOBS WITH DAPR CRON BINDING

Add these new methods (MarkOverdueClaims, GetYesterdaysDueClaims) to the fake implementation for class FakeClaimsManager.cs so the project "**BenefitsManager.Backend.Bff. Api**" builds successfully.

6.4.4 Add Action Methods to the Backend Web API Project

Add a new file, "**OverdueClaimsController**", under the controllers folder in the project "**BenefitsManager.Backend.Bff.Api**" as shown below. We are using Dapr service-to-service invocation API to call the methods **api/overdueclaims** and **api/overdueclaims/markoverdue** from the backend background processor.

```
using BenefitsManager.Common.Models;
using Microsoft.AspNetCore.Mvc;

namespace BenefitsManager.Backend.Bff.Api.Controllers
{
    [Route("api/overdueclaims")]
    [ApiController]
    public class OverdueClaimsController : ControllerBase
    {
        private readonly ILogger<OverdueClaimsController> _logger;
        private readonly IClaimsManager _claimsManager;

        public OverdueClaimsController(ILogger<OverdueClaims
        Controller> logger, IClaimsManager tasksManager)
        {
            _logger = logger;
            _claimsManager = tasksManager;
        }
```

```
    [HttpGet]
    public async Task<IEnumerable<ClaimModel>> Get()
    {
        return await _claimsManager.GetYesterdays
        DueClaims();
    }

    [HttpPost("markoverdue")]
    public async Task<IActionResult> Post([FromBody]
    List<ClaimModel> overdueClaimsList)
    {
        await _claimsManager.MarkOverdueClaims(overdue
        ClaimsList);

        return Ok();
    }
  }
}
```

6.4.5 Add Cron Binding Configuration

Create a new file called "containerapps-scheduled-cron.yaml" under the aca-components folder. This file will be used to update the Azure Container App environment and enable the Cron binding.

```
componentType: bindings.cron
version: v1
metadata:
  - name: schedule
    value: "5 0 * * *" # Everyday at 12:05am
scopes:
  - Benefitsmanager-Backend-Processor
```

CHAPTER 6   ACA WITH DAPR BINDINGS AND SCHEDULED JOBS WITH DAPR CRON BINDING

> **POINT TO NOTE**
>
> The name of the binding is not part of the file metadata. We are going to set the name of the binding to the value "ScheduledClaimManager" when we update the Azure Container Apps environment.

6.5 Deploy Backend API and Backend Background Processor Projects to ACA

6.5.1 Build Both Projects' App Images and Push Them to ACR

To deploy to ACA, we must build and deploy both application images to ACR, just as we did in previous chapters. We can use the same powershell console using the below code (ensure that you are in the correct directory):

```
$BE_BFF_API_NAME="ca-benefitsmanager-bff-api"
$AZURE_CONTAINER_REGISTRY_NAME="crbenefitsmanagerz416"

az acr build `
--registry $AZURE_CONTAINER_REGISTRY_NAME `
--image "benefitsmanager/$BE_BFF_API_NAME" `
--file 'BenefitsManager.Backend.Bff.Api/Dockerfile' .

$BACKEND_SERVICE_NAME="claimsmanager-backend-processor"
az acr build `
--registry $AZURE_CONTAINER_REGISTRY_NAME `
--image "benefitsmanager/$BACKEND_SERVICE_NAME" `
--file 'BenefitsManager.Processor.Backend.Svc/Dockerfile' .
```

6.5.2 Add the Cron Dapr Component to the ACA Environment

Run the following command to add the Cron Dapr component defined in the containerapps-scheduled-cron.yaml file:

```
# Cron binding component
az containerapp env dapr-component set `
--name $ENVIRONMENT --resource-group $RESOURCE_GROUP `
--dapr-component-name scheduledclaimsmanager `
--yaml '.\aca-components\containerapps-scheduled-cron.yaml'
```

6.5.3 Deploy New Revisions of the Backend API and Backend Background Processor to Azure Container Apps

We need to update the Azure container app hosting the backend API and backend background processor with a new revision so our code changes are available for the end users. Run the PowerShell script below:

```
# Update Backend API App container app and create a new revision
az containerapp update `
--name $BACKEND_API_NAME `
--resource-group $RESOURCE_GROUP `
--revision-suffix v$TODAY-2

# Update Backend Background Processor container app and create a new revision
az containerapp update `
--name $BACKEND_SERVICE_NAME `
--resource-group $RESOURCE_GROUP `
--revision-suffix v$TODAY-2
```

CHAPTER 6   ACA WITH DAPR BINDINGS AND SCHEDULED JOBS WITH DAPR CRON BINDING

The service **ScheduledClaimsManager** that will be triggered by the Cron job on certain intervals is hosted in the ACA service ACA-Processor Backend. It is highly recommended that background periodic jobs are hosted in an Azure container app with one single replica, as you don't want your background periodic job to run on multiple replicas trying to do the same thing. This, in fact, would be a limitation that could call for a separate Azure Container App Jobs implementation as we typically want for API/service to scale.

From the Azure portal, you can now open the log streams of the Azure container app hosting the ACA-Processor Backend and check the logs generated when the Cron job is triggered.

6.6 Azure Container Apps Jobs

Azure Container Apps has two types of resources: apps and jobs. Apps are long-running services that respond to HTTP requests or events. Jobs are tasks that run to completion and can be triggered by a schedule or an event.

Jobs can also be triggered programmatically. This makes them a good fit for implementing asynchronous processing in an HTTP API. The API can start a job execution to process the request and return a response immediately. The job can then take as long as it needs to complete the processing. The client can poll a status endpoint on the app to check if the job has completed and get the result.

There are different job trigger types that determine how the job is started:

- **Manual:** These jobs are triggered on demand.
- **Schedule:** These jobs are triggered at specific times, and we can also run them repeatedly at a given interval using Cron schedule.

- **Event:** These jobs are triggered based on an event like a message arriving in a queue or an update to a storage blob.

We can use Azure CLI or Azure portal for creating jobs. The example below shows how we can create a job named *job1* in a resource group named *myresourcegroup* and a container apps environment named *myenv* using the command line:

```
az containerapp job create --name "job1" --resource-group "<myresourcegroup>"  --environment "<myenv>" --trigger-type "Manual" --replica-timeout 1800 --image "<deployable image to ACA>" --cpu "0.25" --memory "0.5Gi"
```

For more details about ACA jobs, refer to Microsoft's official documentation here: https://learn.microsoft.com/en-us/azure/container-apps/jobs?tabs=azure-cli.

6.7 Summary

In this chapter, we examined Dapr binding blocks and their integration with external systems. We updated the Backend Processor service to interact with Azure Storage Queues and Blobs and modified the code to integrate Azure Key Vault for managing secrets. Additionally, we explored Cron bindings and created a new controller, "**ScheduledClaimsManagerController**," to trigger the endpoints.

We also explored Azure Container Apps jobs and various trigger types that can be utilized to create different job types for performing repetitive tasks. Additionally, we updated and revised previously deployed backend APIs and background processors to run on Azure Container Apps.

CHAPTER 7

Monitoring and Observability

In the previous chapters, we have successfully created all the components in the reference architecture and deployed them to Azure Container Apps. In this chapter, we will accomplish four objectives:

- Learn how Azure Container Apps integrate with Application Insights to examine application telemetry.
- Configure Application Insights for microservices.
- Deploy updated background processor, API, and UI projects to Azure.
- Understand how telemetry data is visualized.

7.1 Azure Container Apps and Application Insights

In this chapter, we will explore how we can configure ACA and ACA environment with Application Insights, which will provide a holistic view of our container apps health, performance metrics, logs data, various telemetries, and traces. ACA does not support auto-instrumentation for Application Insights, so in this chapter, we will be focusing on how we can integrate Application Insights into our microservice application.

7.1.1 Application Insights Overview

Application Insights is an offering from Azure Monitor that empowers us to monitor all ACAs under the same Container App Environment and collect telemetry about the workload services. Furthermore, it supports us in understanding the usage of the services and users' engagement via integrated analytics tools.

The term "telemetry" refers to the information gathered to monitor our application, which can be classified into three distinct groups:

1. **Distributed Tracing:** Distributed Tracing allows for visibility into the communication between services participating in distributed transactions. For instance, when the frontend web application interacts with the backend API application to add or retrieve information. An application map of how calls flow between services is very important for any distributed application.

2. **Metrics:** This offers a view of a service's performance and its use of resources. For instance, it helps in monitoring the CPU and memory usage of the backend background processor and identifying when it is necessary to scale up the number of replicas.

3. **Logging:** This provides insights into how code is executed and if errors have occurred.

In Chapter 2, we have already provisioned a workspace-based Application Insights instance and configured it for the ACA environment by setting the property --dapr-instrumentation-key. We presume that you have already set up an instance of Application Insights that is available for use across the three container apps.

7.2 Installing Application Insights SDK into the Three Microservice Applications

7.2.1 Install the Application Insights SDK Using NuGet

Our next step is to incorporate the Application Insights SDK into the three microservices, which is a uniform procedure.

To incorporate the SDK, use the NuGet reference below in the csproj file of the Backend API project. You may locate the csproj file in the project directory **BenefitsManager.Backend.Bff.Api**.

BenefitsManager.Backend.Bff.Api.csproj

```xml
<Project Sdk="Microsoft.NET.Sdk.Web">

  <PropertyGroup>

    <TargetFramework>net9.0</TargetFramework>

    <Nullable>enable</Nullable>

    <ImplicitUsings>enable</ImplicitUsings>

  </PropertyGroup>
  <ItemGroup>
    <PackageReference Include="Dapr.AspNetCore" Version="1.14.0" />
    <PackageReference Include="Microsoft.ApplicationInsights.AspNetCore" Version="2.22.0" />
    <PackageReference Include="Microsoft.AspNetCore.OpenApi" Version="9.0.0" />
  </ItemGroup>
```

```xml
<ItemGroup>
   <ProjectReference Include="..\BenefitsManager.Common.Models\
   BenefitsManager.Common.Models.csproj" />
 </ItemGroup>
</Project>
```

BenefitsManager.Processor.Backend.Svc.csproj

```xml
<Project Sdk="Microsoft.NET.Sdk.Web">

 <PropertyGroup>

   <TargetFramework>net9.0</TargetFramework>

   <Nullable>enable</Nullable>

   <ImplicitUsings>enable</ImplicitUsings>

 </PropertyGroup>
 <ItemGroup>
   <PackageReference Include="Dapr.AspNetCore"
   Version="1.14.0" />
   <PackageReference Include="Microsoft.ApplicationInsights.
   AspNetCore" Version="2.22.0" />
   <PackageReference Include="Microsoft.AspNetCore.OpenApi"
   Version="9.0.0" />
 </ItemGroup>

 <ItemGroup>
   <ProjectReference Include="..\BenefitsManager.Common.Models\
   BenefitsManager.Common.Models.csproj" />
 </ItemGroup>
</Project>
```

BenefitsManager.Frontend.WebPortal.Ui.csproj

```xml
<Project Sdk="Microsoft.NET.Sdk.Web">

 <PropertyGroup>

   <TargetFramework>net9.0</TargetFramework>

   <Nullable>enable</Nullable>

   <ImplicitUsings>enable</ImplicitUsings>

 </PropertyGroup>
 <ItemGroup>
   <PackageReference Include="Dapr.AspNetCore"
   Version="1.14.0" />
   <PackageReference Include="Microsoft.ApplicationInsights.
   AspNetCore" Version="2.22.0" />
 </ItemGroup>
 <ItemGroup>
   <ProjectReference Include="..\BenefitsManager.Common.Models\
   BenefitsManager.Common.Models.csproj" />
 </ItemGroup>
</Project>
```

7.2.2 Set RoleName Property in All the Services

For each of the three projects, we will add a new file to each project's root directory.

    BenefitsManager.Backend.Bff.Api ➤ AppInsightsTelemetry Initializer.cs

```csharp
using Microsoft.ApplicationInsights.Channel;
using Microsoft.ApplicationInsights.Extensibility;
```

CHAPTER 7 MONITORING AND OBSERVABILITY

```
namespace BenefitsManager.Backend.Bff.Api
{
    public class AppInsightsTelemetryInitializer :
    ITelemetryInitializer
    {
        public void Initialize(ITelemetry telemetry)
        {
            if (string.IsNullOrEmpty(telemetry.Context.Cloud.
            RoleName))
            {
                //set custom role name here
                telemetry.Context.Cloud.RoleName =
                "benefitsmanager-backend-api";
            }
        }
    }
}
```

BenefitsManager.Processor.Backend.Svc ➤ AppInsightsTelemetry Initializer.cs

```
using Microsoft.ApplicationInsights.Channel;
using Microsoft.ApplicationInsights.Extensibility;

namespace BenefitsManager.Processor.Backend.Svc
{
    public class AppInsightsTelemetryInitializer :
    ITelemetryInitializer
    {
        public void Initialize(ITelemetry telemetry)
        {
            if (string.IsNullOrEmpty(telemetry.Context.Cloud.
            RoleName))
```

CHAPTER 7 MONITORING AND OBSERVABILITY

```
            {
                //set custom role name here
                telemetry.Context.Cloud.RoleName =
                "benefitsmanager-backend-processor";
            }
        }
    }
}
```

BenefitsManager.Frontend.WebPortal.Ui ➤ AppInsightsTelemetry Initializer.cs

```
using Microsoft.ApplicationInsights.Channel;
using Microsoft.ApplicationInsights.Extensibility;

namespace BenefitsManager.Frontend.WebPortal.Ui
{
    public class AppInsightsTelemetryInitializer :
    ITelemetryInitializer
    {
        public void Initialize(ITelemetry telemetry)
        {
            if (string.IsNullOrEmpty(telemetry.Context.Cloud.
            RoleName))
            {
                //set custom role name here
                telemetry.Context.Cloud.RoleName =
                "benefitsmanager-frontend-webapp";
            }
        }
    }
}
```

CHAPTER 7   MONITORING AND OBSERVABILITY

> **POINT TO NOTE**
>
> The only difference between each file on the three projects is the RoleName property value. Application Insights will utilize this property to recognize the elements on the application map. Additionally, it will prove beneficial for us in case we want to filter through all the warning logs produced by the backend API service. Therefore, we will apply the benefitsmanager-backend-api value for filtering purposes.

Next, we need to register for this AppInsightsTelemetryInitializer class in Program.cs in each of the three projects.

BenefitsManager.Backend.Bff.Api --> Program.cs

```
using BenefitsManager.Common.Models;
using BenefitsManager.Backend.Bff.Api.Services;
using Microsoft.AspNetCore.Http.HttpResults;
using Microsoft.AspNetCore.Mvc;
using Microsoft.ApplicationInsights.Extensibility;
using BenefitsManager.Backend.Bff.Api;

var builder = WebApplication.CreateBuilder(args);

// Learn more about configuring OpenAPI at https://aka.ms/aspnet/openapi
builder.Services.AddOpenApi();

//Add Dapr client
builder.Services.AddDaprClient();

// Add services to the container.
builder.Services.AddApplicationInsightsTelemetry();
builder.Services.Configure<TelemetryConfiguration>((o) => {
```

```
        o.TelemetryInitializers.Add(new AppInsightsTelemetry
        Initializer());
});

builder.Services.AddSingleton<IClaimsManager,
ClaimsStoreManager>();
//builder.Services.AddSingleton<IClaimsManager,
FakeClaimsManager>();

var app = builder.Build();

// Configure the HTTP request pipeline.
if (app.Environment.IsDevelopment())
{
    app.MapOpenApi();
}

app.UseHttpsRedirection();

app.MapGet("/api/claims", async ([FromQuery(Name = "userId")]
string userId, IClaimsManager claimsManager) =>
    TypedResults.Ok(await claimsManager.GetClaimsByCreatorAsync
    (userId)))
    .WithName("GetClaimsByCreator")
    .Produces<List<ClaimModel>>();

app.MapGet("/api/claims/{claimId}", async ([FromRoute] Guid
claimId, IClaimsManager claimsManager) =>
    await claimsManager.GetClaimByIdAsync(claimId)
        is ClaimModel claim ? Results.Ok(claim) : Results.
        NotFound())
            .WithName("GetClaimById")
            .Produces<ClaimModel>()
            .Produces<NotFound>();
```

```
app.MapPost("/api/claims", async ([FromBody] ClaimAddModel 
claimModel, IClaimsManager claimsManager) => 
{ 
    var claimId = await claimsManager.CreateNewClaimAsync
            (claimModel.Merchant, 
            claimModel.ClaimedAmount, 
            claimModel.PurchaseDate, 
            claimModel.CategoryCode, 
            claimModel.Description, 
            claimModel.ReceiptPath, 
            claimModel.CreatedBy); 

    return Results.Created($"/api/claims/{claimId}", claimId); 
}).WithName("CreateNewClaim") 
.Produces<Created<Guid>>(); 

app.MapPut("/api/claims/{claimId}", async ([FromRoute] Guid 
claimId, [FromBody] ClaimUpdateModel claimModel, IClaimsManager 
claimsManager) => 
    await claimsManager.UpdateClaimAsync(claimId, 
    claimModel.Merchant, 
    claimModel.ClaimedAmount, 
    claimModel.PurchaseDate, 
    claimModel.CategoryCode, 
    claimModel.Description, 
    claimModel.ReceiptPath) 
    is bool updateResult ? Results.Ok(updateResult) : Results.
    NotFound() 
).WithName("UpdateClaim") 
.Produces<Ok<bool>>() 
.Produces<NotFound>();
```

CHAPTER 7   MONITORING AND OBSERVABILITY

```
app.MapPut("/api/claims/{claimId}/status", async
([FromRoute] Guid claimId, [FromBody] ClaimStatusUpdateModel
claimStatusUpdateModel, IClaimsManager claimsManager) =>
    await claimsManager.UpdateClaimStatusAsync(claimId,
    claimStatusUpdateModel.ApprovedAmount,
    claimStatusUpdateModel.NewStatus,
    claimStatusUpdateModel.Comment,
    claimStatusUpdateModel.SetBy)
    is bool updateResult ? Results.Ok(updateResult) : Results.
    NotFound()
).WithName("UpdateClaimStatus")
 .Produces<Ok<bool>>()
 .Produces<NotFound>();

app.MapDelete("/api/claims/{claimId}", async ([FromRoute] Guid
claimId, IClaimsManager claimsManager) =>
    await claimsManager.DeleteClaimAsync(claimId)
    ? Results.Ok() : Results.NotFound()
).WithName("DeleteClaim")
 .Produces<Ok>()
 .Produces<NotFound>();

app.Run();
```

BenefitsManager.Processor.Backend.Svc ➤ Program.cs

```
using Microsoft.ApplicationInsights.Extensibility;

namespace BenefitsManager.Processor.Backend.Svc
{
    public class Program
    {
        public static void Main(string[] args)
```

```csharp
{
    var builder = WebApplication.CreateBuilder(args);
    // Add services to the container.
    builder.Services.AddApplicationInsightsTelemetry();
    builder.Services.Configure<TelemetryConfiguration
    >((o) => {
        o.TelemetryInitializers.Add(new AppInsights
        TelemetryInitializer());
    });

    builder.Services.AddControllers().AddDapr();

    builder.Services.AddControllers();
    // Learn more about configuring Swagger/OpenAPI at
    https://aka.ms/aspnetcore/swashbuckle
    builder.Services.AddEndpointsApiExplorer();
    builder.Services.AddSwaggerGen();

    var app = builder.Build();
    // Configure the HTTP request pipeline.
    if (app.Environment.IsDevelopment())
    {
        app.UseSwagger();
        app.UseSwaggerUI();
    }

    app.UseHttpsRedirection();

    app.UseAuthorization();

    app.UseCloudEvents();

    app.MapControllers();

    app.MapSubscribeHandler();
```

```
            app.Run();
        }
    }
}
```

BenefitsManager.Frontend.WebPortal.Ui ➤ Program.cs

```
using BenefitsManager.Common.Models;
using BenefitsManager.Frontend.WebPortal.Ui.Services;
using BenefitsManager.Frontend.WebPortal.Ui.Components;
using Microsoft.ApplicationInsights.Extensibility;
using BenefitsManager.Frontend.WebPortal.Ui;

var builder = WebApplication.CreateBuilder(args);

// Add services to the container.
builder.Services.AddApplicationInsightsTelemetry();
builder.Services.Configure<TelemetryConfiguration>((o) => {
    o.TelemetryInitializers.Add(new AppInsights
    TelemetryInitializer());
});

builder.Services.AddRazorComponents()
    .AddInteractiveServerComponents();

// Add Dapr client
builder.Services.AddDaprClient();

builder.Services.AddScoped(sp => new HttpClient { BaseAddress =
new Uri("http://localhost:5103") });
builder.Services.AddScoped<ClaimsService>();

builder.Logging.SetMinimumLevel(LogLevel.Debug);
builder.Logging.AddConsole();

var app = builder.Build();
```

```
// Configure the HTTP request pipeline.
if (!app.Environment.IsDevelopment())
{
    app.UseExceptionHandler("/Error", createScopeFor
       Errors: true);
    // The default HSTS value is 30 days. You may want to
       change this for production scenarios, see https://aka.
       ms/aspnetcore-hsts.
    app.UseHsts();
}

app.UseHttpsRedirection();

app.UseStaticFiles();
app.UseAntiforgery();

app.MapRazorComponents<App>()
    .AddInteractiveServerRenderMode();

app.Run();
```

7.2.3 Set the Application Insights Instrumentation Key

In Chapter 6, we've used the Dapr Secret Store to store connection strings and keys. In this chapter, we will demonstrate how we can use another approach to secrets in Container Apps.

We need to set the Application Insights instrumentation key so that the projects are able to send telemetry data to the Application Insights instance. We are going to set this via secrets and environment variables once we redeploy the Container Apps and create new revisions. Locally, we can set it in each appsettings.json file. We can get the value of the

Application insights instrumentation key during deployment via az commands in Chapters 2, 3, and 5 for backend API, frontend UI, and background processor apps, respectively.

$APPINSIGHTS_INSTRUMENTATIONKEY

    appsettings.json

```
{
 // Configuration removed for brevity
 "ApplicationInsights": {
   "InstrumentationKey": "<Application Insights Key here for
                          local development>"
 }
}
```

With this step completed, we have done all the changes needed. Let's now deploy the changes and create new ACA revisions.

7.3 Deploy Services to ACA and Create New Revisions

7.3.1 Add Application Insights Instrumentation Key As a Secret

Let's create a secret named appinsights-key on each container app that contains the value of the Application Insights instrumentation key:

```
az containerapp secret set --name $BE_BFF_API_NAME --resource-
group $RESOURCE_GROUP ` --secrets "appinsights-
key=$APPINSIGHTS_INSTRUMENTATIONKEY"
```

```
az containerapp secret set --name $FE_WEB_UI_NAME --resource-
group $RESOURCE_GROUP ` --secrets "appinsights-
key=$APPINSIGHTS_INSTRUMENTATIONKEY"

az containerapp secret set --name $BACKEND_SERVICE_NAME
--resource-group $RESOURCE_GROUP ` --secrets "appinsights-
key=$APPINSIGHTS_INSTRUMENTATIONKEY"
```

7.3.2 Build New Images and Push Them to ACR

As we did before, we are required to build and push the images of the three applications to ACR. By doing so, they will be prepared to be deployed in ACA.

To accomplish this, continue using the same PowerShell console and paste the code below (make sure you are on the right folder of each project):

```
# Build Backend API on ACR and Push to ACR
az acr build `
--registry $AZURE_CONTAINER_REGISTRY_NAME `
--image "benefitsmanager/$BE_BFF_API_NAME" `
--file 'BenefitsManager.Backend.Bff.Api/Dockerfile' .

# Build Backend Service on ACR and Push to ACR
az acr build `
--registry $AZURE_CONTAINER_REGISTRY_NAME `
--image "benefitsmanager/$BACKEND_SERVICE_NAME" `
--file 'BenefitsManager.Processor.Backend.Svc/Dockerfile' .

# Build Frontend Web App on ACR and Push to ACR
az acr build `
--registry $AZURE_CONTAINER_REGISTRY_NAME `
--image "benefitsmanager/$FE_WEB_UI_NAME" `
--file 'BenefitsManager.Frontend.WebPortal.Ui/Dockerfile' .
```

7.3.3 Deploy New Revisions of the Services to ACA and Set a New Environment Variable

We need to update all three container apps with new revisions so that our code changes are available for end users.

> **POINT TO NOTE**
>
> Notice how we used the property --set-env-vars to set a new environment variable named ApplicationInsights__InstrumentationKey. Its value is a secret reference obtained from the secret appinsights-key we added in Section 7.3.1.

```
# Update Backend API App container app and create a new revision
az containerapp update `
--name $BE_BFF_API_NAME `
--resource-group $RESOURCE_GROUP `
--revision-suffix v$TODAY-5 `
--set-env-vars "ApplicationInsights__InstrumentationKey=secretref:appinsights-key"

# Update Frontend Web App container app and create a new revision
az containerapp update `
--name $FE_WEB_UI_NAME `
--resource-group $RESOURCE_GROUP `
--revision-suffix v$TODAY-5 `
--set-env-vars "ApplicationInsights__InstrumentationKey=secretref:appinsights-key"
```

```
# Update Backend Background Service container app and create a
new revision
az containerapp update `
--name $BACKEND_SERVICE_NAME `
--resource-group $RESOURCE_GROUP `
--revision-suffix v$TODAY-5 `
--set-env-vars "ApplicationInsights__InstrumentationKey=secret
ref:appinsights-key"
```

With those changes in place, you should start seeing telemetry coming to the Application Insights instance provisioned. Let's review Application Insights' key dashboards and panels in the Azure portal.

7.4 Visualizing Telemetry Data

7.4.1 Distributed Tracing via Application Map

Open the Azure portal, and navigate to Application Insights resource. On the left side pane, expand the Investigate node and click on Application Map. This will help us spot any performance bottlenecks or failure hotspots across all our services of our distributed microservice application. Each node on the map represents an application component (service) or its dependencies and has a health KPI and alerts status.

You will see, for example, how the backend API with RoleName benefitsmanager-backend-api is depending on the Cosmos DB instance, showing the number of calls and average time to service these calls. The application map is interactive so you can select a service/component and drill down into details. Figure 7-1 shows how to navigate and generate application map view from Application Insights resource within the Azure portal.

CHAPTER 7   MONITORING AND OBSERVABILITY

For example, when we drill down into the Dapr State node to understand how many times the backend API invoked the Dapr Sidecar state service to Save/Delete state, you will see results about number of calls and the time it takes to complete in ms.

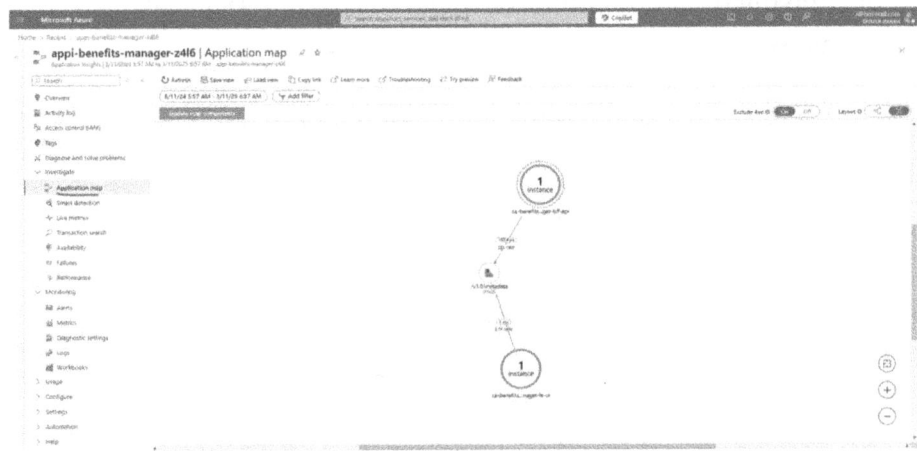

Figure 7-1. Application map view from Application Insights inside the Azure portal

POINT TO NOTE

It will take some time for the application map to fully populate.

7.4.2 Monitor Production Application Using Live Metrics

This is one of the key monitoring panels. It provides you with near real-time (one-second latency) status of your entire distributed application. We have the ability to observe both the successes and failures of our system, monitor any exceptions occurring, and trace them in real time.

Additionally, we can monitor the live servers (including replicas) and track their CPU and memory usage, as well as the number of requests they are currently handling.

These live metrics provide very powerful diagnostics for our production microservice application. Figure 7-2 shows some of the incoming requests to the system.

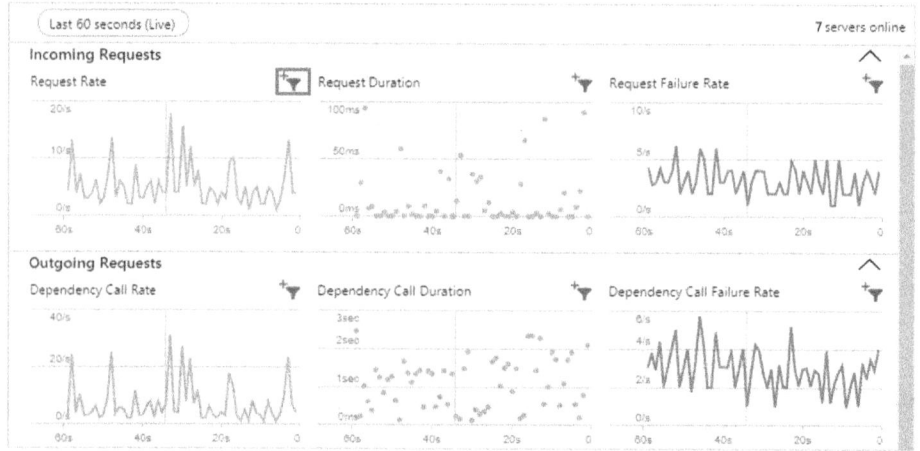

Figure 7-2. Live metrics from App Insights in the Azure portal

7.4.3 Logs Search Using Transaction Search

Transaction search in Application Insights will help us find and explore individual telemetry items, such as exceptions, web requests, or dependencies as well as any log traces and events that we've added to the application. Figure 7-3 shows how to navigate to Transaction Search view inside Application Insights resource from the Azure portal.

CHAPTER 7 MONITORING AND OBSERVABILITY

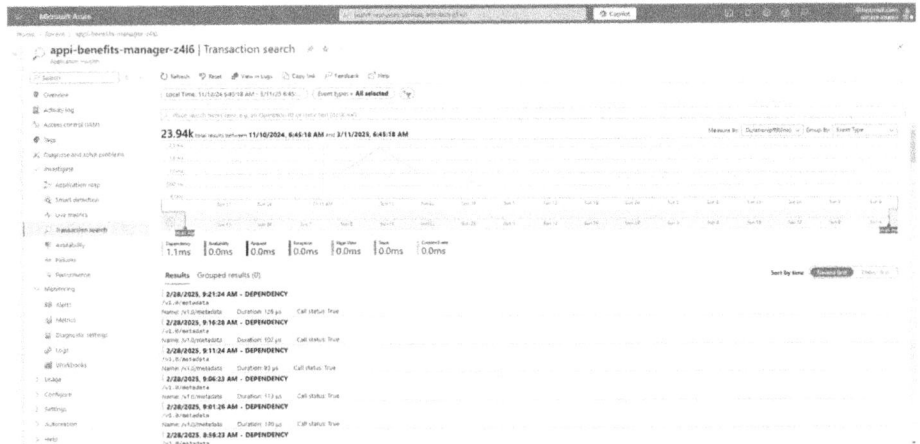

Figure 7-3. *Navigating to Transaction Search Application Insights view from the Azure portal*

For example, if we want to see all the event types of type Request for the cloud RoleName benefitsmanager-backend-api in the past 24 hours, we can use the transaction search dashboard to do this. See how the filters are set, and the results are displayed nicely. We can drill down on each result to have more details and know what telemetry was captured before and after, a very useful feature when troubleshooting exceptions and reading logs. We can also use KQL to filter logs as per your needs. Figure 7-4 shows transaction search logs generated via KQL query.

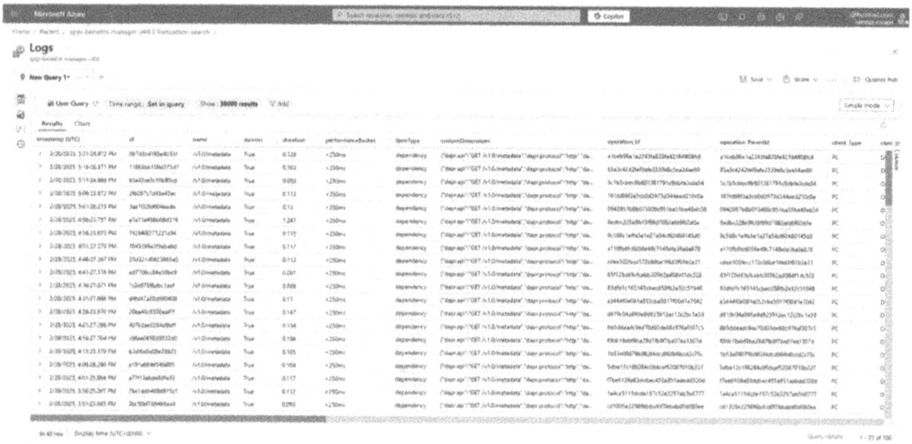

CHAPTER 7   MONITORING AND OBSERVABILITY

Figure 7-4. Transaction search logs query generated from App Insights in the Azure portal

7.4.4 Failures and Performance Panels

The Failure panel enables us to assess the frequency of failures across various operations, which assists us in prioritizing our efforts toward the ones that have the most significant impact.

The Performance panel displays performance details for the different operations in our system. By identifying those operations with the longest duration, we can diagnose potential problems or best target our ongoing development to improve the overall performance of the system. Figure 7-5 shows how to navigate to Failures view inside Application Insights resource from the Azure portal.

CHAPTER 7   MONITORING AND OBSERVABILITY

Figure 7-5. *Failures view from App Insights in the Azure portal*

7.5 Summary

In this chapter, we have learned how Azure Container Apps integrate with Application Insights to examine application telemetry; configured Application Insights for all the microservices; deployed updated background processor, API, and UI projects to Azure; and understood how telemetry data is visualized.

In the next chapter, we will discuss how to create autoscaling rules with KEDA.

CHAPTER 8

Kubernetes Event-Driven Autoscaler (KEDA)

In this chapter, we will discuss ACA's autoscaling behaviors with KEDA. The learning objectives for this chapter include the following:

- Understand Azure Container Apps scaling behaviors.
- Learn about the kubernetes-based Event-driven Autoscaler (KEDA).
- Create a scaling rule for the backend background processor project.
- Test scaling of the backend background processor.

8.1 Azure Container Apps Scaling Behaviors

In this chapter, we will explore how we can configure autoscaling rules in container apps. The autoscaling feature is one of the key features of any serverless hosting platform because it empowers your application to adjust dynamically. This means your application can automatically handle higher (or lower) workloads, ensuring your system maintains its availability and performance.

Azure Container Apps support horizontal scaling, also known as scaling out and scaling in. Respectively, when demand increases, Azure Container Apps can add (scale out) replicas (new instances of the container app), allowing the system to handle more requests in parallel. Each request is processed by a single instance, but having multiple replicas ensures that the workload is distributed efficiently. Ideally, this keeps the workload per instance somewhat consistent with that instance's capacity. Conversely, when demand decreases, Azure Container Apps will remove (scale in) unutilized or underutilized replicas according to your configured scaling rule. With this consumption-oriented approach, you pay only for the replicas provisioned at any time. You can also configure the scaling rule to scale to zero replicas, resulting in no costs being incurred when your container app scales down to zero. However, be aware that scaling to zero for critical workloads is advised against, as it can introduce latency when restarting the service from scratch to handle new requests.

For more details about cost/billing, please refer to https://learn.microsoft.com/en-us/azure/container-apps/billing.

8.1.1 Scaling Triggers

Azure Container Apps supports different scaling triggers including

- **HTTP Traffic:** Scaling based on the number of concurrent HTTP requests handled by each replica of your container app. For more details, refer to https://learn.microsoft.com/en-us/azure/container-apps/scale-app?pivots=azure-cli#http.

- **CPU or Memory Usage:** Scaling based on the amount of CPU utilized or memory consumed by a replica. For more details, refer to https://learn.microsoft.com/en-us/azure/container-apps/scale-app?pivots=azure-cli#memory.

- **Azure Storage Queues:** Scaling based on the number of messages in Azure Storage Queue.

- **Event Driven Using KEDA:** Scaling based on event triggers, such as the number of messages in Azure Service Bus Topic or the number of blobs in Azure Blob Storage container. For more details, refer to https://keda.sh/.

As mentioned in Chapter 1, Azure Container Apps utilize different open source technologies, including KEDA, which facilitates tasks such as event-driven autoscaling. KEDA is installed by default when you provision your container app, so you don't need to install it. We only need to enable and configure scaling rules for our container app.

8.2 Overview of Kubernetes Event-Driven Autoscaler (KEDA)

KEDA stands for **Kubernetes Event-Driven Autoscaler**. It is an open source project initially started by Microsoft and Red Hat to allow any Kubernetes workload to benefit from the event-driven architecture model. Prior to KEDA, horizontally scaling a Kubernetes deployment was achieved through the **Horizontal Pod Autoscaler** (HPA). The HPA relies on resource metrics such as memory and CPU to determine when additional replicas should be deployed. In an enterprise application, there may be additional external metrics that we want to use to scale our application, such as the length of a Kafka topic log, an Azure Service Bus Queue, or metrics obtained from a Prometheus query. In short, scaling considerations are likely to be increasingly complex as your applications and ecosystem grow. KEDA offers more than 50 scalers to pick from based on your business needs. KEDA exists to fill this gap and provides a framework for scaling based on events in conjunction with HPA scaling based on CPU and memory. Figure 8-1 shows how KEDA works with Kubernetes Horizontal Pod Autoscaler, external event sources, and Kubernetes' etcd data store.

KEDA enables dynamic scaling through two key components. The **KEDA operator** manages workload scaling between 0 and N instances, supporting resources like Jobs, StatefulSets, and custom resources with a /**scale** subresource. The **Metrics Server** provides external metrics to HPA for autoscaling based on events such as Azure Event Hubs or Kafka messages. For more details, refer to `https://keda.sh/`.

CHAPTER 8 KUBERNETES EVENT-DRIVEN AUTOSCALER (KEDA)

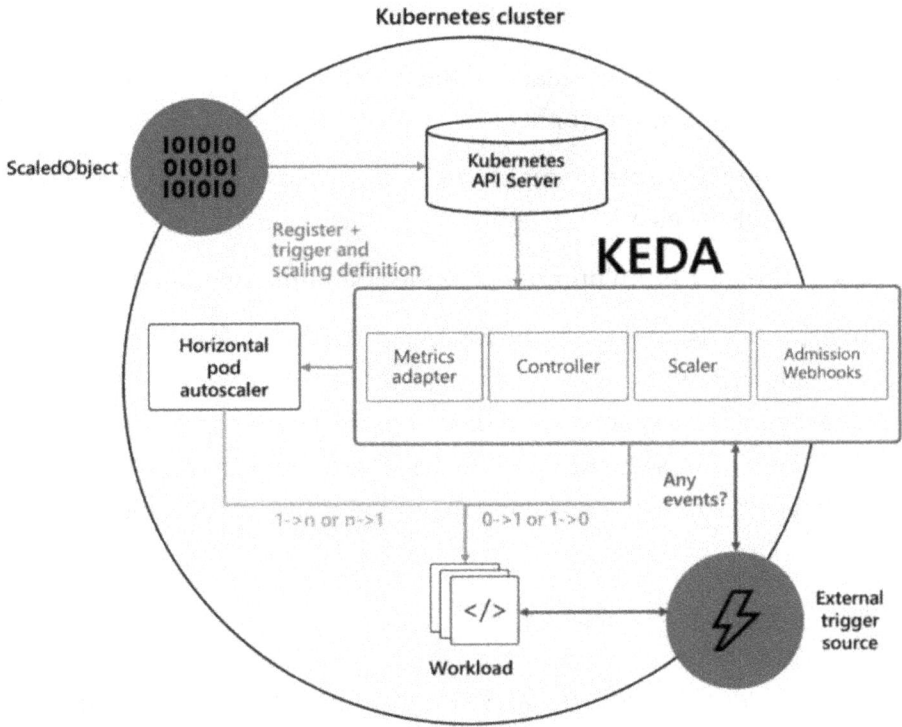

Figure 8-1. KEDA works in conjunction with HPA and other components (Courtesy: https://keda.sh/)

8.3 Configure Scaling Rule in the Backend Background Processor Project

8.3.1 KEDA Azure Service Bus Scaler

In this section, let's configure our **backend background processor**, *BenefitsManager-backend-processor*, to scale out based on the number of messages in the Azure Service Bus Topic, *claimsavedtopic*. When the service experiences heavy load and a single replica is insufficient, we want the container app to create additional replicas to distribute message processing efficiently.

Our requirements for scaling the backend processor are as follows:

- For every ten messages on the Azure Service Bus Topic, scale out by one replica.

- When there are no messages on the topic, scale in to a single replica.

- The maximum number of replicas should not exceed **5**.

To achieve this, we look at the KEDA Azure Service Bus Scaler (for more details, refer to https://keda.sh/docs/2.0/scalers/azure-service-bus/). This specification describes the azure-servicebus trigger for Azure Service Bus Queue or Topic. Let's take a look at the YAML file below that contains a generic template for the KEDA specification:

```
triggers:
- type: azure-servicebus
  metadata:
    # Required: queueName OR topicName and subscriptionName
    queueName: queueName
    # or
    topicName: topicName
    subscriptionName: subscriptionName
    # Optional, required when pod identity is used
    namespace: service-bus-namespace
    # Optional, can use TriggerAuthentication as well
    connectionFromEnv: SERVICEBUS_CONNECTIONSTRING_ENV_NAME
    # This must be a connection string for a queue itself,
    and not a namespace level (e.g. RootAccessPolicy)
    connection string
    # Optional
    messageCount: "5" # Optional. Count of messages to trigger
    scaling on. Default: 5 messages
```

```
cloud: Private # Optional. Default: AzurePublicCloud
endpointSuffix: servicebus.airgap.example # Required when
cloud=Private
```

Let's explore the contents of the YAML file:

- The property type is set to **azure-servicebus**. Each KEDA scaler specification file has a unique type.

- One of the properties, queueName or topicName, should be provided. In our case, it will be topicName, and we will use the value **claimsavedtopic**.

- The property subscriptionName will be set to use **benefitsmanager-backend-processor.** This represents the subscription associated with the topic. Not needed if we are using queues.

- The property **connectionFromEnv** will be set to reference a secret stored in our container app. We will not use the Azure Service Bus shared access policy (connection string) directly. The shared access policy will be stored in the Container App secrets, and the secret will be referenced here. Please note that the Service Bus shared access policy needs to be of type Manage. It is required for KEDA to be able to get metrics from Service Bus and read the length of messages in the queue or topic.

- The property **messageCount** is used to decide when scaling out should be triggered. In our case, it will be set to **5**.

- The property **cloud** represents the name of the cloud environment that the service bus belongs to.

Azure Container Apps has its own proprietary schema to map a KEDA Scaler template to its own when defining a custom scale rule. You can define this scaling rule via Container Apps ARM templates, YAML manifest, Azure CLI, or from the Azure portal. In this chapter, we will cover how to do it from the Azure CLI.

POINT TO NOTE

The KEDA scaler for Azure Service Bus supports different authentication mechanisms such as Pod Managed Identity, Azure AD Workload Identity, and shared access policy (connection string). When using KEDA with Azure Container Apps, the only supported authentication mechanism is Connection Strings. However, the ACA product team worked on their backlog that involves enabling KEDA Scale with Managed Identity (for details, refer to this issue: https://github.com/microsoft/azure-container-apps/issues/592).

8.3.2 Create a New Secret in the Container App

Let's now create a secret named svcbus-connstring in our **benefitsmanager-backend-processor** container app. This secret will contain the value of Azure Service Bus shared access policy (connection string). To accomplish this, run the following commands in the Azure CLI to get the connection string, and then add this secret using the second command:

```
# List Service Bus Access Policy RootManageSharedAccessKey
$SERVICE_BUS_CONNECTION_STRING = az servicebus namespace authorization-rule keys list `
--name RootManageSharedAccessKey `
--resource-group $RESOURCE_GROUP `
```

```
--namespace-name $SERVICE_BUS_NAMESPACE_NAME `
--query primaryConnectionString `
--output tsv

# Create a new secret named 'svcbus-connstring' in backend
processor container app
az containerapp secret set `
--name $BACKEND_SERVICE_NAME `
--resource-group $RESOURCE_GROUP `
--secrets "svcbus-connstring=$SERVICE_BUS_CONNECTION_STRING"
```

8.3.3 Create a Custom Scaling Rule from Azure CLI

If you have created a new secret, we are now ready to add a new custom scaling rule to match the business requirements. To accomplish this, we need to run the below Azure CLI command.

> **POINT TO NOTE**
>
> You might need to upgrade the extension if you are on an older version of az containerapp, which didn't allow you to create a scaling rule from CLI. To update the extension, you can run the command az extension update --name containerapp inside your PowerShell terminal.

```
az containerapp update `
--name $BACKEND_SERVICE_NAME `
--resource-group $RESOURCE_GROUP `
--min-replicas 1 `
--max-replicas 5 `
--revision-suffix v$TODAY-6 `
```

CHAPTER 8   KUBERNETES EVENT-DRIVEN AUTOSCALER (KEDA)

```
--scale-rule-name "topic-msgs-length" `
--scale-rule-type "azure-servicebus" `
--scale-rule-auth "connection=svcbus-connstring" `
--scale-rule-metadata "topicName=$SERVICE_BUS_TOPIC_NAME" `
                     "subscriptionName=$SERVICE_BUS_TOPIC_
                     SUBSCRIPTION" `
                     "namespace=$SERVICE_BUS_
                     NAMESPACE_NAME" `
                     "messageCount=5" `
                     "connectionFromEnv=svcbus-connstring"
```

- Setting the minimum number of replicas to **1**. This means that this container app could be scaled in to a single replica if there are no new messages on the topic.

- Setting the maximum number of replicas to **5**. This means that this container app will not exceed more than **5** replicas regardless of the number of messages on the topic.

- Setting a friendly name for the scale rule **topic-msgs-length**, which will be visible in the Azure portal.

- Setting the scale rule type to **azure-servicebus**. This is important to tell KEDA which type of scalers our container app is configuring.

- Setting the authentication mechanism to type connection and indicating which secret reference will be used. In our case, **svcbus-connstring**.

- Setting the metadata dictionary of the scale rule. Those match the metadata properties in the KEDA template we discussed earlier.

About Setting Minimum Replicas to 0: We can set the minimum number of replicas to zero to avoid any charges when the backend processor is not processing any message from Azure Service Bus Topic, but this will impact running the other features within this backend processor such as the periodic Cron job as well as the external input binding and output bindings. We are configuring the minimum number of replicas to one, ensuring that a backend processor instance is always running and capable of handling tasks, even if there are no messages being received by the Azure Service Bus Topic.

When the single replica of the backend processor is not doing anything, it will be running in an idle mode. When the replica is in idle mode, usage is charged at a reduced idle rate. A replica enters an active mode and is charged at the active rate when it is starting up and when it is processing requests. For more details about the ACA pricing, refer to this link: https://azure.microsoft.com/en-us/pricing/details/container-apps/.

8.4 Testing Scaling Rules

8.4.1 End-to-End Test to Generate Several Messages

If you have successfully set the above rules, we are now ready to test out our Azure Service Bus Scaling Rule. To produce a high volume of messages, you can utilize the Service Bus Explorer located within your Azure Service Bus namespace. Navigate to Azure Service Bus, choose your topic/subscription, and then select the Service Bus Explorer option. To get the number of current replicas of service **benefitsmanager-backend-processor**, we could run the command below; this should run a single replica as we didn't load the service bus topic yet.

CHAPTER 8   KUBERNETES EVENT-DRIVEN AUTOSCALER (KEDA)

```
az containerapp replica list `
--name $BACKEND_SERVICE_NAME `
--resource-group $RESOURCE_GROUP `
--query [].name
```

The message structure our backend processor expects is similar to the JSON shown below. So copy this message and click the Send messages button, paste the message content, set the content type to application/json, check the Repeat Send check box, select 10000 messages, and put an interval of 1 ms between them. This ensures that we are sending high volume at short intervals so that the single replica container app cannot absorb and process quickly enough and will consequently need to scale out. Finally click Send when you are ready.

```
{
    "data": {
      "claimId": "59E029B1-1621-45A1-8263-A77AA7758FAE",
      "merchant": "Merchant-10",
      "claimedAmount": 80,
      "approvedAmount": null,
      "purchaseDate": 1733201907427,
      "category": {
        "categoryCode": "CAT004",
        "parentCategoryName": "Fitness Activities",
        "categoryName": "Gym"
      },
      "description": "Random description2",
      "statusLog": [
        {
          "status": 0,
          "comment": "",
          "setBy": {
```

```
      "id": "323a3afe-711f-4aa6-80d0-f848d24a5340",
      "email": "user3@mail.com",
      "name": "User-3"
    },
    "ts": 1733450307427
  }
],
"currentStatus": 0,
"receiptPath": "https://storage.blob.core.windows.net/
claims/63105a50-e295-4619-8708-c790601c976d/receipt.pdf",
"createdBy": {
  "id": "323a3afe-711f-4aa6-80d0-f848d24a5340",
  "email": "user3@mail.com",
  "name": "User-3"
},
"createdOn": 1733450307427,
"modifiedOn": null
  }
}
```

If all is set up correctly, five replicas will be created based on the number of messages we generated into the topic. There are various ways to verify this:

- You can re-run the Azure CLI command above to list the name of replicas (command from this subsection).

- You can verify this from the container apps console tab where you will see those replicas in the drop-down list.

8.5 Summary

In this chapter, we explored the Azure Container Apps scaling behaviors and Kubernetes Event-Driven Autoscaler (KEDA) and its architecture. We also discussed how to configure and create a scaling rule for the backend background processor project. We finally verified it end to end by sending a high number of messages to see how new replicas are created to handle the load. As your applications and ecosystem grow, scaling becomes increasingly complex, and that's where KEDA exists to fill this gap by providing a framework to scale based on events.

Index

A

ACA, *see* Azure Container Apps (ACA)
ACA-Processor Backend service, 176, 178–180, 187
AddDapr registers, 158
AKS, *see* Azure Kubernetes Service (AKS)
Application Insights, 50–52, 218
Application Insights instrumentation key, 230–232
　build and push the images, 232
　as secret, 231, 232
Application map, 234, 235
app.MapSubscribeHandler(), 159
app.UseCloudEvents(), 158
Authentication, 20
Autoscaling, 11, 19
Azure Container Apps (ACA), 55, 136, 140, 143, 218
　Application Insights, 218
　Application Insights Instrumentation Key, 231, 232
　Benefits Manager Backend, 26–28
　architectures, 4
　background processing, 9
　building and publishing, 83, 84
　capabilities, 1, 2, 171
　comparisons, 12–14
　container orchestration, 1
　deploying, 84
　deployment, 53, 54
　development environment set up, 24, 25
　with Distributed Application Runtime (Dapr), 93, 94
　environment, 5
　environment variable, 233, 234
　input and output binding component files, 199–201
　jobs, 214, 215
　key features and benefits, 10–12
　microservices, 3, 7–11
　new revisions, 172, 173
　pricing and plans, 17, 18
　public API endpoints, 8
　published API, 55
　reference architecture, 20
　revision mode, 5
　serverless paradigm, 2
　use cases, 6–10, 16, 17
　workload profile, 3

INDEX

Azure Container Registry (ACR), 19, 52, 55, 80
    frontend web App, 138, 139
    service, 25, 26
Azure Cosmos DB, 110
    Azure Container Apps (ACA), 140
    backend and frontend application, 133–135
    built-in Cosmos DB role, 137, 138
    component file, 130–133
    with Container Apps, 136–138
    placeholders with values, 126, 127
Azure Infrastructure, 48–50
Azure Key Vault
    ACA Dapr Secrets Store, 198, 199
    backend processor, 196, 197
    creation, 195, 196
    secrets, 197, 198
Azure Kubernetes Service (AKS), 14
    concepts and management, 14
    control, 14
    VNet integration, 15
Azure Log Analytics workspace, 50–52
Azure Service Bus
    Dapr Pub/Sub Component, 172
    namespace, 163–165
    Pub/Sub API, 165–170
Azure Storage Account, 182
Azure Storage Queues, 176, 178, 179, 183, 186, 188
Azure Virtual Network, 5

B

Backend API, 162, 163
Backend Background Processor
    New Azure Container, 171, 172
    root directory, 170
Backend Background Service, 159
Backend processor, 196, 197
Backend service project
    ACA Processor, 150
    ASP.NET Core, 150
    docker configuration, 150–153
    models addition, 153
Backend Web API container App, 85–87
Backend Web API Project, 205–210
    action methods, 210, 211
    Azure Container Apps (ACA), 213, 214
    configuration, 211, 212
    Cron Dapr component, 213
    deploying to ACA, 212, 213
Background processor, 162
Background Processor Project
    Azure Container Apps (ACA), 213, 214
    client SDK, 189–192
    Cron Dapr component, 213
    deploying to ACA, 212, 213
    event handler, 183–185

INDEX

input binding component file, 185–187
output binding component file, 187–189
Background tasks, 17
BenefitsManager-Backend-Bff-Api, 135
BenefitsManager-Backend-Processor, 198
Benefits Manager microservice application, 93, 94
Bindings, 91
Bindings building block, 177
Blazor framework, 59, 60
   all-in-one stack, 60
   arbitrary UI events, 60
   change-based rendering, 60
   component-based architecture, 59
   cross-platform development, 61
   JavaScript, 61
   server-side and client-side rendering, 60
   Visual Studio and Visual Studio Code, 61
Built-in monitoring, 11

C

CI/CD, *see* Continuous Integration/Continuous Deployment (CI/CD)
ClaimDetails.razor, 76–78
ClaimModel class, 153
ClaimModel.cs file, 63
claimsavedtopic, 148, 162
ClaimsService class, 65–68
ClaimsStoreManager, 124, 125
ClaimsStoreManager.cs, 162, 163
Cloud Native Computing Foundation (CNCF), 90
CNCF, *see* Cloud Native Computing Foundation (CNCF)
Code structure
   Docker configuration, 44–47
   Enums, 28
   models, 28–31
   program configuration, 41–43
   services folder, 31–41
Command-line terminal, 153
Consumer startup, 157–162
Consumption plan, 17
Consumption profile, 3
Container Apps, 5
Containerization, 1
Containers, 6, 13
Continuous Integration/Continuous Deployment (CI/CD), 26
Cosmos DB Built-in Data Contributor, 136
Cost optimization, 2
Cron binding, 201
   backend web API project, 205–210
   configuration binding, 201, 202
   Cron Dapr component, 213
   endpoint addition, 203–205

INDEX

D

Dapr, *see* Distributed Application Runtime (Dapr)
DaprClient, 124, 125
Dapr component schema file, 138
Dapr Cron Binding
    bindings building block, 178–182
    external system, 176, 177
    input and output binding component files, 199–201
Dapr integration, 7, 12
Dapr Pub/Sub pattern, 143–145
    API endpoint, 154–157
    backend service project, 150–163
    SDK Client, 153
    testing, 145–149
Dapr sidecar, 179
Dapr State Management building block, 110–118
dapr-statestore-cosmos.yaml file, 132, 133
Dedicated profile, 3
Deployment model, 13
Developer command prompt, 125
Distributed Application Runtime (Dapr), 89, 175
    ACA Web-Frontend configuration, 100–104
    ACA Web running, 104–106
    ACA Web testing, 106, 107
    with Azure Container Apps (ACA), 93, 94
    backend API configuration, 97–100
    bindings building block, 178–182
    building blocks, 91–93
    challenges, 90
    Client SDK, 118–125
    frontend and backend container apps, 140–141
    graduated maturity level, 90
    incubating maturity level, 90
    key/value pairs, 111
    local development machine, 94–97
    publisher-Subscriber (Pub/Sub) pattern, 143–145
    register, 157–162
    State Management API, 110–118
    VS Code, 107–110
    See also Dapr Cron Binding
Distributed tracing, 218
Docker configuration, 44–47, 80–82, 150–153
Docker Desktop, 58
Dockerfile, 151
Docker image, 53, 83, 84
Dotnet 9.0, 24, 58

E

Enums, 28
Event-driven applications, 16
Event-driven processing, 8
Event handler, 183–185

INDEX

F

FakeClaimsManager.cs, 119
Frontend Blazor Web
      Application, 57, 68
    ClaimModel.cs Class, 63
    ClaimsService class, 65–68
    components, 68–78
    components layout, 64–66
    creation, 62, 63
    development environment
        set up, 58
    Docker configuration, 80–82
    program configuration, 78–80
    See also Blazor framework

G

Geo-replication, 25
GetYesterdaysDueClaims
        method, 208

H

Home.razor
        component, 72–76
HTTP requests, 47, 48

I

IaaS, *see* Infrastructure as a
        Service (IaaS)
Infrastructure as a
        Service (IaaS), 3
Integrated authentication, 25

J

Jobs, 9, 10, 92, 214, 215

K

Key Vault Secrets User, 196
Kubernetes, 1, 2, 11, 14

L

Linux, 44, 151
Live metrics, 236, 237
Local Redis Cache, 115–118
Log Analytics workspace, 5
Logging, 218
Logs search, 236–238

M

Metadata, 130
Metrics, 218
Microservices, 7–11, 13, 16, 18,
    26, 90, 176
Microservices Apps
    Application Insights
        Instrumentation Key,
        230, 231
    NuGet, 219–221
    RoleName Property, 221–230
mTLS, *see* Mutual
        authentication (mTLS)
Mutual authentication
        (mTLS), 94

INDEX

N

.NET developers, 100
Network configurations, 26
NewClaim.razor component, 68–72
NuGet APPs, 219–221
NuGet package, 153

O

Open-source technologies, 12
Output binding, 189–192

P

PaaS, *see* Platform as a Service (PaaS)
Platform as a Service (PaaS), 13
POST request, 112–115
PowerShell, 125, 139
    commands, 128
    console, 140
    script, 171
    terminal, 98, 125
    windows, 142
PowerShell 7.0, 24, 58
primaryMasterKey, 129, 130
ProcessClaimAndStore, 185, 191
PublishClaimSavedEvent, 162
Publisher-Subscriber (Pub/Sub), 173
publish/subscribe messaging, 91
Pub/Sub, *see* Publisher-Subscriber (Pub/Sub)
Pub-Sub pattern, 156
Pub/Sub model, 144–146

Q

Queue-based scaling, 8

R

Redis, 163
Redis Xplorer, 115
Replica, 6
Resource allocation, 2
Resource-based scaling, 9
Revision mode, 5
RoleName Property, 221

S

Scaling, 13
secretstoreakv, 198
Self-hosted mode, 97
Serverless, 15
Serverless simplicity, 11
Server-rendered web apps, 61
Service-to-service communication, 91
State Management, 91
Statestore, 115
State Store Management
    ACA-Dapr Component file, 138, 139
    Azure Cosmos DB, 125–138
    Backend API Project, 118
    component file, 130–133
    concrete implementation, 119–124
Subscribe Handler, 157–162

INDEX

T

Telemetry data, 217, 218
    distributed
        tracing, 234, 235
    failure panel, 238, 239
    live metrics, 236
    logs search, 236–238
    performance
        panels, 238, 239

U

URL value, 131
User interface, 69–71

V

vaultName value, 198
Virtual network (VNet)
    integration, 15
Visual Studio, 58, 61, 62, 153
Visual Studio (VS) Code, 24, 44–46
    .http files, 47, 48
VS Code, 134

W, X, Y, Z

WeatherForecast.cs, 150
Well-known endpoint, 155
Workflows, 92

GPSR Compliance

The European Union's (EU) General Product Safety Regulation (GPSR) is a set of rules that requires consumer products to be safe and our obligations to ensure this.

If you have any concerns about our products, you can contact us on

ProductSafety@springernature.com

In case Publisher is established outside the EU, the EU authorized representative is:

Springer Nature Customer Service Center GmbH
Europaplatz 3
69115 Heidelberg, Germany

www.ingramcontent.com/pod-product-compliance
Lightning Source LLC
LaVergne TN
LVHW022037260326
834688LV00060B/767

9798868814853